THE
LONGING
IN ME

THE
LONGING
IN ME

A Study in the Life of David

STUDY GUIDE

SIX SESSIONS

SHEILA
WALSH

WITH CHRISTINE M. ANDERSON

NELSON
BOOKS

An Imprint of Thomas Nelson

The Longing in Me Study Guide

© 2016 by Sheila Walsh

Published in Nashville, Tennessee, by Nelson Books, an imprint of Thomas Nelson. Nelson Books and Thomas Nelson are registered trademarks of HarperCollins Christian Publishing, Inc.

Author is represented by the literary agency of Alive Communications, Inc., 7680 Goddard Street, Suite 200, Colorado Springs, CO 80902, www.alivecommunications.com.

In some instances, names, dates, locations, and other identifying details have been changed to protect the identities and privacy of those mentioned in the DVD and study guide.

Unless otherwise indicated, Scripture quotations are taken from the *Holy Bible, New Living Translation.* © 1996, 2004, 2007, 2013 by Tyndale House Foundation. Used by permission of Tyndale House Publishers, Inc., Carol Stream, Illinois 60188. All rights reserved.

Scripture quotations marked ESV are from the *English Standard Version,* Copyright © 2001. The *ESV* and *English Standard Version* are trademarks of Good News Publishers.

Scripture quotations marked MSG are from *The Message.* Copyright © by Eugene H. Peterson 1993, 1994, 1995, 1996, 2000, 2001, 2002. Used by permission of Tyndale House Publishers, Inc.

Scripture quotations marked NASB are from *New American Standard Bible*®. Copyright © 1960, 1962, 1963, 1968, 1971, 1972, 1973, 1975, 1977, 1995 by The Lockman Foundation. Used by permission. (www.Lockman.org)

Scripture quotations marked NIV are from the Holy Bible, *New International Version*®, *NIV*®. Copyright © 1973, 1978, 1984, 2011 by Biblica, Inc.® Used by permission of Zondervan. All rights reserved worldwide. www.zondervan.com. The *NIV* and *New International Version* are trademarks registered in the United States Patent and Trademark Office by Biblica, Inc.®

Thomas Nelson titles may be purchased in bulk for educational, business, fundraising, or sales promotional use. For information, please e-mail SpecialMarkets@ThomasNelson.com.

ISBN 978-0-310-68486-2

16 17 18 19 20 /DCI/ 20 19 18 17 16 15 14 13 12 11 10 9 8 7 6 5 4 3

Printed in the United States of America

Contents

How to Use This Guide

Group Size

The Longing in Me video study is designed to be experienced in a group setting such as a Bible study, Sunday school class, or any small group gathering. To ensure everyone has enough time to participate in discussions, it is recommended that large groups break up into smaller groups of four to six people each.

Materials Needed

Each participant should have her own study guide, which includes notes for video segments, directions for activities and discussion questions, as well as personal studies to deepen learning between sessions.

Timing

The time notations—for example (17 minutes)—indicate the *actual* time of video segments and the *suggested* times for each activity or discussion. For example:

Individual Activity: What I Want to Remember (2 minutes)

Adhering to the suggested times will enable you to complete each session in one hour. If you have a longer meeting, you may wish to allow more time for discussion and activities. You may also opt to devote two meetings rather than one to each session. In addition to allowing discussions to be more spacious, this has the added advantage of allowing group members to read related chapters in *The Longing in Me* book and to complete the personal study between meetings. In the second meeting, devote the time allotted for watching the video to discussing group members' insights and questions from their reading and personal study.

Practice

Each session ends with a suggested application activity for group members to complete on their own between sessions. Although the activity is completed outside of the group meeting, reading through the practice before concluding the meeting to clarify any questions and to make sure everyone is on board is a good idea.

Facilitation

Each group should appoint a facilitator who is responsible for starting the video and for keeping track of time during discussions and activities. Facilitators may also read questions aloud and monitor discussions, prompting participants to respond and ensuring that everyone has an opportunity to participate.

Personal Studies

Maximize the impact of the curriculum with additional study between group sessions. Every personal study includes reflection questions, Bible study, and a guided prayer activity. You'll get the most out of the study by setting aside about thirty minutes between sessions for personal study, as well as additional time to complete the practice activities.

Longing to Be Chosen

If I find in myself a desire which no experience in
this world can satisfy, the most probable explanation
is that I was made for another world.

C. S. Lewis, *Made for Heaven*

Welcome!

Welcome to Session 1 of *The Longing in Me.* If this is your first time together as a group, take a moment to introduce yourselves to one another before watching the video. Then let's begin!

Video: Longing to Be Chosen (19 minutes)

Play the video segment for Session 1. As you watch, use the outline provided to follow along or to take additional notes on anything that stands out to you.

Notes

> "We shall not cease from exploration
> And the end of all our exploring
> Will be to arrive where we started
> And know the place for the first time."
>
> *— T. S. Eliot*

The human heart longs for closure and understanding. It longs to change the ending of those things in our lives that have scarred us badly.

David was known as "a man after God's own heart," yet he made choices that cost him and others dearly.

We all long to be chosen. But when those longings are unmet, what do we do? Even more, when those longings *are* met, why is there an even greater ache that remains? … No matter how great your longing is for God, it will never, ever compare to His longing for you.

"God chose the things despised by the world, things counted as nothing at all, and used them to bring to nothing what the world considers important" (1 Corinthians 1:28). These words exactly describe David, the man God chose to be king over Israel (see 1 Samuel 13:14).

We're drawn by charisma more than character. But charisma cracks under pressure, while character doesn't.

The God who created you has chosen you as His beautifully loved daughter. Because of that, you can take rejections in your life in stride.

Group Discussion (39 minutes)

Take a few minutes to talk about what you just watched.

1. What part of the teaching had the most impact on you?

_____

_____

_____

Betrayed by Longing

2. Sheila pointed out that our high school years often rank near the top of the scale when it comes to intensity and longing. She described herself as an "awkward girl" in this season of her life and shared a painful story about how "popular girls" used her longings to torment her. As you reflect on this same era in your own life, which of the following high school stereotypes come closest to describing you? Place a check mark next to your top two or three.

☐ Prep/preppie	☐ Dweeb/dork	☐ Metalhead
☐ Nerd	☐ Popular (A-list)	☐ Loner
☐ Star athlete	☐ Popular (B-list)	☐ Invisible girl
☐ Loser	☐ Cheerleader	☐ Rebel
☐ Punk	☐ Band geek	☐ Depressed girl
☐ Goth	☐ Freak	☐ Fat girl
☐ Good girl	☐ Indie girl	☐ Skinny girl
☐ Mean girl	☐ Slacker	☐ Drama nerd
☐ Fashionista	☐ Artist/musician	☐ Super-spiritual girl
☐ Overachiever	☐ Angry girl	☐ Other: _____
☐ Stoner	☐ Party girl	

- Stereotypes can be true to a point, but they can also obscure truth. In what ways do the words and phrases you checked represent something genuinely true about your high school self? In what ways do they also obscure something true about who you were?

- How would you describe the deeper or hidden longings behind the words and phrases you checked? For example, the deeper longing behind being the overachiever might be a need for significance, affirmation, or self-worth. The hidden longing behind being the fat or skinny girl might be a need to be seen as desirable or to be noticed for something other than body size.

- In what ways might the longings you described also be an expression of the desire to be seen and chosen?

- Sheila described the devastation she felt when she realized what the popular girls at the dance had done. She was angry at everyone, but most of all, she said, "I was angry with myself . . . my longing had betrayed me." In what ways, if any, do you relate to this response? How would you describe the purpose of punishing or blaming ourselves (or our longings) when we are hurt by someone else?

Heart Choices

3. As the youngest of eight sons, David was up against a big stereotype—the no-account little brother. And while it was true that David was last by birth order and therefore considered least by most people—including his father and brothers—the stereotype also obscured a larger truth about who David really was: "a man after [God's] own heart" (1 Samuel 13:14). We get a better understanding of what this statement about David's heart really means by listening in on a heated conversation between the prophet Samuel and King Saul, who has blatantly disregarded a command from God:

> Samuel said, "What is this you have done?"
>
> Saul replied, "I saw my men scattering from me, and you didn't arrive when you said you would, and the Philistines are at Micmash ready for battle. So I said, 'The Philistines are ready to march against us at Gilgal, and I haven't even asked for the LORD's help!' So I felt compelled to offer the burnt offering myself before you came."
>
> "How foolish!" Samuel exclaimed. "You have not kept the command the LORD your God gave you. Had you kept it, the LORD would have established your kingdom over Israel forever. But now your kingdom must end, for the LORD has sought out a man after his own heart. The LORD has already appointed him to be the leader of his people, because you have not kept the LORD's command." (1 Samuel 13:11–14)

When deep need alone is the driving force behind our choices, we're almost guaranteed to end up in a place we'd rather not be—a ditch or worse. Seeing how this plays out with Saul is not difficult. First, he rationalizes his behavior by pointing out his dire circumstances, and then he skirts responsibility for his foolish choices by blaming Samuel. Saul essentially says, *Look, things around here have been going downhill fast. If you'd shown up when you were supposed to, I wouldn't have been forced to take matters into my own hands. I didn't want to do it, but you left me no choice.*

Now contrast this illustration of Saul's heart with the apostle Paul's description of David:

> God removed Saul and replaced him with David, a man about whom God said, "I have found David son of Jesse, a man after my own heart. He will do everything I want him to do." (Acts 13:22)

- Based on the passages from 1 Samuel 13 and Acts 13, how would you characterize the differences between Saul's heart and David's heart?

  _____

  _____

  _____

- What does it mean in practical terms to be a person "after God's own heart"? In other words, in the course of everyday life, what thoughts or behaviors are a tip-off that you are or are not living as a person after God's own heart?

  _____

  _____

  _____

- Saul is actually somewhat of a sympathetic character in this story. Given the same circumstances, most of us wouldn't consider it unreasonable or sinful to show fear or to take action. The problem came when Saul put his deep needs in the driver's seat. Saul *did* have a choice—he could have looked to *God* to meet his needs. Instead, he chose to meet his needs on his own terms without regard for God.

  _____

  _____

  _____

- In what ways do you relate to Saul? In what circumstances are you most likely to make choices that effectively say to God, *Look, I have a hard situation here, and since You're not coming through for me in the way I'd hoped or as quickly as I'd hoped, I don't have any choice but to take matters into my own hands?*

  _____

  _____

  _____

- How would you describe the ditch you end up in—the familiar place you'd rather not be—when your deep needs or longings are in the driver's seat of your choices? What is the lesson you can't seem to learn about this area of your life?

_____

_____

_____

_____

4. In 1 Samuel 13 we learn something about the difference between Saul's heart and David's heart. In 1 Samuel 16 we learn about the difference between another pair of hearts—the human heart and God's heart. In rejecting Eliab, David's visibly impressive eldest brother, God says to Samuel:

> The LORD doesn't see things the way you see them. People judge by outward appearance, but the LORD looks at the heart.
> (1 Samuel 16:7)

Understanding the meaning of the word _heart_ helps us to grasp the significance of this statement. We tend to think of the heart primarily in connection with emotions, but the ancient Hebrew understanding of heart was both broader and richer. To speak of the heart was to refer to the "entire inner life of a person"[1]—everything we might describe as psychological, spiritual, intellectual, and emotional. In its purest state, the heart was the bright and unique essence of who God created a person to be.

- It was no secret to God that David would one day make choices that cost him and others dearly, and yet He still chose David and deemed him "a man after my own heart." How does the ancient Hebrew concept of heart help you understand something about what God saw when He looked at David's heart? About what He sees when He looks at your heart?

_____

_____

_____

_____

- In what ways does this truth that the Lord looks at the heart both challenge you and encourage you?

5. In the video, Sheila described how God has already chosen you—a choice based on His heart of love and longing for you. "No matter how great your longing is for God," Sheila said, "it will never, ever compare to His longing for you."

    Take a moment to reflect on both your longing for God and on God's longing for you. How would you describe your awareness of both?

    - *Your longing for God.* When are you most aware of your longing for God? Is your longing for God the strongest it has ever been, the weakest, or somewhere between? Why?

    - *God's longing for you.* Author Brennan Manning writes, "Christians find it easier to believe that God exists than that God loves them."[2] To what degree might this be true of you? When are you, or when have you been, most aware of God's longing for you?

Hearts Together

6. In addition to studying together, it's important to also be aware of how God is at work among you — especially in how you relate to one another and share your lives throughout the study. In each session, you will have many opportunities to speak life-giving — and life-challenging — words and to listen to one another deeply.

   As you anticipate the next several weeks of learning together in community, what request would you like to make of the group? For example, how do you hope other members will challenge you or encourage you? Use one or more of the sentence starters below, or your own statement, to help the group understand the best way to be a good friend to you throughout this study. As each person responds, use the two-page chart that follows to briefly note what is important to that person and how you can be a good friend to her during your discussions and times together.

   I'd like you to consistently challenge me about . . .

   It really helps me to engage in a group when . . .

   I tend to withdraw or feel anxious when . . .

   You can help me to take this study seriously by . . .

   In our discussions, the best thing you could do for me is . . .

Name	The Best Way I Can Be a Good Friend to This Person Is ...

Name	The Best Way I Can Be a Good Friend to This Person Is . . .

Individual Activity: What I Want to Remember (2 minutes)

Complete this activity on your own.

1. Briefly review the video outline and any notes you took.

2. In the space below, write down the most significant thing you gained in this session—from the teaching, activities, or discussions.

What I want to remember from this session . . .

_____

_____

_____

_____

Practice: Look for Longing

Each session in *The Longing in Me* study includes a practice for you to complete between sessions. Although the practice is completed on your own and outside of group time, reading through the practice description before concluding your meeting each week is a good idea. In some cases, activities may require preparation or setting aside time each day to complete. To get the most out of the practice, it's important not to hurry or try to complete activities at the last minute.

The practice for this week is to increase your awareness of longings—both your own longings and God's longing for you. While some desires and longings are obvious or could even be overwhelming, others are sometimes shy or hidden from view. But every desire has within it the potential to teach us something about our longings for God and about God's longing for us.

To be aware of something is to be attentive to it—to listen, watch, and observe. To be attentive to our longings—especially the shy ones—we must be respectful, which means we observe without making judgments and without shaming. The invitation of this practice is to set aside time to simply notice, which is the first step toward gaining understanding. Here are two options for ways to be attentive to longings between now and your next group meeting.

☐ ***Set aside fifteen minutes at the beginning or end of each day this week to reflect on the previous twenty-four hours.*** Divide the day into three parts—morning, afternoon, and evening. For each part of the day, look for any signs of desire or longing at work. Evidence might be obvious, or it could be found in something very small or subtle. For example, you might notice a desire either to be with or to avoid a certain person, to acquire a possession, to eat something, to change your circumstances. Or you might consistently find your mind dwelling on something you are either looking forward to or dreading—the upcoming weekend, a romantic date, a difficult conversation, a medical appointment. Desires are contained within all of these things.

Use a journal or pad of paper to write down at least one or two observations about your desires for each part of the day—morning, afternoon, and evening. For example, *I'm really looking forward to having time off. I hope the medical report brings good news. I don't want to feel lonely anymore. I wish I could sense God's presence right now.* If you find it challenging to make these observations after the fact, consider keeping your pad of paper with you and writing down your observations as they happen throughout the day. At the end of the week, review your daily observations. What stands out most to you about your desires? In what ways do these desires reflect something true about you? About your longing for God? About God's longing for you?

☐ ***Set aside thirty minutes to identify your longings and desires by giving yourself permission to dream.*** At some point in life, most of us wish we had a magic wand we could wave to swiftly and painlessly change our lives. If you could do this, what would you change—about yourself, your relationships (with God and others), your circumstances, etc.? Use a journal or notepad to write down every desire that comes to mind, however small. And don't rush! Allow at least twenty minutes to ponder what you really want, knowing that some desires may be shy or hidden. Then spend at least ten minutes reflecting on what you wrote. What stands out most to you about your desires? In what ways do these desires reflect something true about you? About your longing for God? About God's longing for you?

Bring your notes to the next group gathering. You'll have a chance to talk about your experiences and observations at the beginning of the Session 2 discussion.

Closing Prayer

Close your time together with prayer.

Personal Study

Read and Learn

Read the introduction and chapter 1 of *The Longing in Me*. Use the space below to note any insights or questions you want to bring to the next group session.

Study and Reflect

The innate longing to be loved and chosen can lead us into very damaging situations.... We know that God loves us, but we can't see God with our eyes or feel His arms around us or hear His audible voice telling us that we are loved. So we look for that kind of love and acceptance in someone [or something] else.

The Longing in Me, pages 6, 11

1. Use the prompts below to briefly identify a few circumstances in which your longing to be loved and chosen led you into damaging situations. They could be situations resulting from your own choices, or from circumstances over which you had little or no control.

    Two of the earliest situations that come to mind are . . .

    _____

    _____

    _____

    Two of the more recent situations that come to mind are . . .

    _____

    _____

    _____

    Sheila writes, "The human heart longs for closure and understanding. In many ways it longs to right the wrongs of childhood . . . to change the ending of something that has scarred us badly" (page xiii). As you reflect on the situations you just identified, how would you describe the "closure and understanding" you hope for, or the ending(s) you're trying to change?

    _____

    _____

    _____

2. Sometimes it helps to understand our longings when we put them in the form of a question. For example, the question behind a longing to be loved might be, *Am I lovable?* The question behind a longing to be chosen might be, *Am I special?* As you consider your responses to question 1, which of the questions in the list on the following page come closest to articulating the longings that either led you into those damaging situations or came about because of them? Place a check mark next to your top two or three.

☐ Am I lovable?

☐ Am I special?

☐ Am I loved unconditionally?

☐ Am I safe?

☐ Do my needs matter?

☐ Will people like me or accept me?

☐ Am I a good person?

☐ Do I belong?

☐ Will I be chosen?

☐ Am I okay?

☐ Am I interesting?

☐ Do I measure up?

☐ Will I be loved if I make a mistake?

☐ Do I matter?

☐ Am I needed?

☐ Is my life meaningful?

☐ Am I worthy of love?

☐ Is it okay to be me?

☐ Am I good enough?

☐ Am I desirable?

☐ Other: _____

In the group session video, Sheila shared the story of Mary, who grew up with an unreliable father. The question behind Mary's longing to be loved was, *Am I enough?* Through her young adult years, her efforts to bring closure to this question led her to repeatedly choose men who didn't keep their word. Over and over again, the only answer to her question seemed to be, *No, I am not enough.* As a result, Mary saw herself as damaged goods—she felt defeated, stuck, and unlovable.

As you reflect on the questions you checked, what answers have you arrived at? How have your attempts to bring closure impacted the way you see yourself?

_____

_____

_____

_____

_____

> The God of the universe has already chosen you and says to
> you, "You are Mine!"
>
> *The Longing in Me*, page 16

3. God sees you—the person you are and the person He created you to be—and He chooses you. That's good news, right? But maybe you find yourself thinking something like this: *There's nothing special about being chosen if everyone is chosen. If God loves us all equally, then I'm just part of the crowd and there isn't anything unique about how God loves me.* Author C. S. Lewis provides a compelling alternative to this line of thinking. Even though God loves all His children *equally*—to infinity and beyond—that doesn't mean God loves us all *the same*. Lewis writes:

> I am considering not how, but why, [God] makes each soul unique.
> If he had no use for all these differences, I do not see why he
> should have created more souls than one....

As part of his reasoning, Lewis references the Lord's compelling promise of an individualized heavenly reward: "I will give to each one a white stone, and on the stone will be engraved a new name that no one understands except the one who receives it" (Revelation 2:17). This is a gift from God that no one in the universe but you will receive! Lewis concludes:

> Each of the redeemed shall forever know and praise some one aspect
> of the Divine beauty better than any other creature can. Why else
> were individuals created, but that God, loving all infinitely, should
> love each differently?... If all experienced God in the same way
> and returned to him an identical worship, the song of the Church
> triumphant would have no symphony, it would be like an orchestra
> in which all the instruments played the same note.[3]

What impact does Lewis's perspective have on your understanding of what it means that God chooses you and loves you differently than He loves anyone else?

If you were to take seriously this truth that you are uniquely loved and chosen by God, what would have to change about the way you see yourself (question 2)? About the way you ask and answer the questions you checked?

_____

_____

_____

4. The Psalms are sometimes referred to as the prayer book of the Bible, and many of the psalms are attributed to David, our biblical companion throughout this study. Read Psalm 63:1–8, a psalm of David when he was in the desert wilderness of Judah. The psalm expresses longing for God as an intense thirst. Pray the psalm through slowly, allowing the words of David to stir your own longing for God. Using the psalm as a reference, use the space below to write your own prayer. Surrender your longings and the questions behind them to God, asking Him to help you find the answers you seek in your relationship with Him. Invite God to show you this week how He loves you uniquely and personally. Thank Him for the promise that His love satisfies "more than the richest feast" (Psalm 63:5).

_____

_____

_____

_____

_____

_____

_____

_____

_____

_____

_____

Longing to Be Protected

We are secure. God is running the show.

Eugene H. Peterson,
A Long Obedience in the Same Direction

Checking In (8 minutes)

A key part of getting to know God better is sharing your journey with others. Before watching the video, briefly check in with one another about your experiences since the last session. For example:

- Briefly share your experience of the Session 1 practice activity, "Look for Longing." What did you learn or experience as you tried to increase your awareness of longings—both your own longings and God's longing for you?

- What insights did you discover in the personal study or in the chapters you read from *The Longing in Me*?

- How did the previous session impact your daily life or your relationship with God?

- What questions would you like to ask the other members of your group?

Video: Longing to Be Protected (19 minutes)

Play the video segment for Session 2. As you watch, use the outline provided to follow along or to take additional notes on anything that stands out to you.

Notes

Even though he seriously messed up many times, King David had an out-loud, honest, vibrant relationship with God. There's something about David's honesty that we need to press into, to dig deep to find.

Young David learned that when everyone else failed him, God would always protect him. In the same way, when our longing is directed toward God, we'll never be left empty and alone. David understood that no matter how big the giant we face right now, God is bigger.

David and Goliath

"God brought me to prison to set me free."

—Pam, inmate in a women's prison

Most of us will never find ourselves in prison, but at times we all feel imprisoned by fear.

Remember, the battle is the Lord's. The ship is His to steer and bring safely home. Your job is to show up and be brave!

Group Discussion (31 minutes)

Take a few minutes to talk about what you just watched.

1. What part of the teaching had the most impact on you?

Seeking Safety

2. The need for safety and protection is a fundamental human need. When we feel threatened, we find it difficult or impossible to function normally until we find some way to either overcome the threat or protect ourselves from it.

    *   How do you tend to respond when you feel unsafe for any reason? Consider your mental, physical, and emotional response. For example:

        My mental response: *My mind is always racing, obsessed with how to get out of the situation or fix the problem.*

        My physical response: *I feel tense and jumpy and can't sleep. My eating patterns change.*

        My emotional response: *Sometimes I shut down completely; other times I cry easily.*

- When you feel unsafe, what kinds of things do you typically do to protect yourself?

- At the beginning of the video, Sheila explained how feeling exposed and unprotected as a child created a longing for protection that eventually led her to make what she described as a disastrous choice to marry the wrong man. What initially felt like safety ultimately left her feeling even more exposed and unprotected, which can happen anytime we direct our longing for protection to someone or something besides God.

  In what ways, if any, do you relate to Sheila's experience of misdirecting her longing for protection? How did your efforts to secure safety and protection ultimately lead you into greater danger, worsen your situation, or damage relationships?

Slaying Giants

Optional Activity: David and Goliath (10 minutes)

If time permits, read together the full story of David and Goliath recorded in 1 Samuel 17:1–50. Go around the group and have each person read four or five verses at a time. As the story is read, pay particular attention to the differences between how David responded and how King Saul and the Israelites responded to the threat posed by Goliath and the Philistines.

3. Sheila used the story of David and Goliath to illustrate how we can rely on God for protection when we face "giants" of our own. Because of his faith in God's protection, David didn't have to be coerced, guilted, or drafted into fighting Goliath — he enthusiastically

volunteered! He knew the dangers, but he didn't obsess about how inadequate he was or dwell on his lack of resources. Instead, he faced the reality of the situation head-on and made a confident choice to engage the enemy.

> "Don't worry about this Philistine," David told Saul. "I'll go fight him!"
>
> "Don't be ridiculous!" Saul replied. "There's no way you can fight this Philistine and possibly win! You're only a boy, and he's been a man of war since his youth."
>
> But David persisted. "I have been taking care of my father's sheep and goats," he said. "When a lion or a bear comes to steal a lamb from the flock, I go after it with a club and rescue the lamb from its mouth. If the animal turns on me, I catch it by the jaw and club it to death. I have done this to both lions and bears, and I'll do it to this pagan Philistine, too, for he has defied the armies of the living God! The LORD who rescued me from the claws of the lion and the bear will rescue me from this Philistine!" (1 Samuel 17:32–37)

David's decision wasn't a blind leap of faith—he didn't naïvely throw himself in harm's way hoping with fingers crossed that God might possibly, somehow show up. His decision was a clear-minded choice to trust that the God who had protected him in the past could be relied on to protect him in the present. Author and pastor Dallas Willard elaborates on the implications this truth has for us:

> We can never understand the life of faith seen in scripture and in serious Christian living unless we drop the idea of faith as a "blind leap" and understand that faith is commitment to action, often beyond our natural abilities, *based upon knowledge of God and God's ways.*[4]

The foundation of David's confidence is what Sheila described as his "spiritual resumé," and what Willard characterizes as "knowledge of God and God's ways." David's decisive response and confident outlook stood in stark contrast to that of King Saul and the Israelites, whose fears had immobilized them for forty days straight and left them "terrified and deeply shaken" (1 Samuel 17:11).

SESSION TWO: LONGING TO BE PROTECTED

- We know from Scripture that King Saul and the Israelites also had strong spiritual resumés — that God had repeatedly protected and provided for them. Given that the Israelites and David were now facing the same terrifying threat, what do you think accounts for the differences in their responses? In other words, why did Goliath mobilize David but immobilize the Israelites?

- One of the ironies about the human need for protection and safety is that most of us require some degree of safety in order to take the legitimate risks required to grow and to meet the ever-changing demands of life. How is this dynamic evident in both David's response and in the responses of King Saul and the Israelites? What might their respective responses reveal about their relationships with God?

- Imagine for a moment that the exchange you read between Saul and David is instead an internal dialogue, the kind of conversation you might have with yourself when you are wrestling with a difficult problem. How would you characterize the discussion? For example, what kinds of things does your internal "Saul" typically say? How does your internal "David" respond? Whose perspective and reasoning are you most likely to follow?

4. Whereas David had what author and pastor Eugene Peterson characterizes as a "God-dominated imagination," King Saul and the Israelites had a "Goliath-dominated imagination."[5] Their view of reality was shaped entirely by the threat they faced. David's view of reality was shaped instead by what he knew to be true about God and God's ways.

- As you consider the giants you've faced (in the past or recently), how would you characterize your view of reality? In what ways was it Goliath-dominated (shaped by your fears)? In what ways was it God-dominated (shaped by your faith)?

  _____

  _____

  _____

- In the situation you just described, how did your view of reality influence your ability to experience safety and protection? To what degree were you able to take legitimate risks to meet the demands of your situation?

  _____

  _____

  _____

5. Perhaps one of the most encouraging insights we can draw from David's story is that his God-dominated imagination—the faith and confidence that enabled him to slay a giant—is something he *learned*, which means we can learn it too. David actually trained himself to think and act this way by pursuing and relying on God in the everyday challenges he faced as a shepherd. This cultivated habit of saturating his mind with God's perspective and then acting on it is similar to what the apostle Paul urged the church at Colosse to develop:

   > Since you have been raised to new life with Christ, set your sights on the realities of heaven, where Christ sits in the place of honor at God's right hand. Think about the things of heaven, not the things of earth. (Colossians 3:1–2)

   The Message offers a fresh perspective on this familiar passage:

   > So if you're serious about living this new resurrection life with Christ, *act* like it. Pursue the things over which Christ presides. Don't shuffle along, eyes to the ground, absorbed with the things right in front of you. Look up, and be alert to what is going on around Christ—that's where the action is. See things from *his* perspective. (Colossians 3:1–2 MSG)

- What parallels do you recognize between the Colossians passage and the David and Goliath story? Specifically, how might Saul and the Israelites illustrate a life focused on the things of earth? How might David illustrate a life focused on the things of heaven?

  _____

  _____

  _____

- Think of an area of everyday life in which you tend to "shuffle along … absorbed with the things right in front of you." How might this area of your life change if you believed without a doubt that God is your protector?

  _____

  _____

  _____

- How do you sense God may be inviting you to learn and train in "resurrection life with Christ," to cultivate a habit of seeing challenges and hardships from God's perspective?

  _____

  _____

  _____

Hearts Together

6. At the end of the Session 1 group discussion, you had the opportunity to make a request of the group and to write down the best ways you could be good friends to one another.

- Briefly restate what you asked for from the group in Session 1. What additions or clarifications would you like to make that would help the group to know more about how to be a good friend to you? As each person responds, add any additional information to the Session 1 chart. (If you were absent from the last session, share your response to Session 1, question 6. Then use the chart to write down what is important to each member of the group.)

  _____

  _____

- In what ways, if any, did you find yourself responding differently to other members of the group in this session based on what they asked for in the previous session? What made that easy or difficult for you to do?

Individual Activity: What I Want to Remember (2 minutes)

Complete this activity on your own.

1. Briefly review the video outline and any notes you took.

2. In the space below, write down the most significant thing you gained in this session—from the teaching, activities, or discussions.

    What I want to remember from this session . . .

Practice: Write Your Spiritual Resumé

The practice this week is to follow David's example and engage in spiritual strength training — to develop your confidence in God as your protector and provider — by writing your spiritual resumé.

Just as a professional resumé provides a summary of job-related experiences and education, a spiritual resumé summarizes God-related experiences and education — your knowledge of God and God's ways. When applying for a job, a professional resumé gives a potential employer evidence of your qualifications. When facing a personal challenge, a spiritual resumé gives you evidence of God's qualifications. This is your foundation for confidence that God will be with you now just as He has been in the past.

- *Set aside twenty to thirty minutes to reflect on your life with God.* If possible, settle into a quiet place where you won't be interrupted. Begin with a minute or two of silence, prayerfully asking God to quiet your mind and your heart. Invite God to help you recall the ways in which He has been there for you in the past — all the evidence of His provision, protection, healing, and grace.

- *Use a journal or a pad of paper to briefly note what comes to mind* — what God has done in you, through you, and for you. You might begin by completing sentence starters like, *God provided for me by . . ., God protected me when . . ., God healed me from . . ., God enabled me to . . .,* and so on. Or, if you find it helpful, you might follow David's "I/the Lord" approach. In reciting his spiritual resumé for King Saul, David first catalogs his personal experience with several "I" statements: "*I* have been taking care of my father's sheep," "*I* go after [the lion or bear]," "*I* . . . rescue the lamb," "*I* catch [the lion or bear] by the jaw and club it to death," "*I* have done this." But then David acknowledges that it is "*the LORD* who rescued me from the claws of the lion and the bear" (1 Samuel 17:34–37, emphasis added). David's statements are also very specific. To convince King Saul that he could fight Goliath and win, David didn't merely say, "God kept me safe while I tended sheep." He said, "God kept me safe while I killed lions and bears — with my bare hands!" Try to write down at least three of your experiences. Here are some examples to get you started:

> *I apologized, and the Lord healed our relationship.*
>
> *I took a risk to go back and finish my degree, and the Lord provided a scholarship.*
>
> *I held my tongue, and the Lord taught me self-control.*
>
> *I surrendered my life to Christ, and the Lord changed me.*
>
> *I started a small business when I lost my job, and the Lord paid my bills.*
>
> *I battled cancer, and the Lord healed me.*
>
> *I cut up my credit cards and stuck to a budget, and the Lord got me out of debt.*

- Once you have documented what God has done, **consider what you now know about God and God's ways because of these experiences.** Use this knowledge to make a declaration of confidence about a current problem or challenge you face. David declared his confidence this way: "The LORD who rescued me from the claws of the lion and the bear will rescue me from this Philistine!" Here are some examples:

  > *The Lord who paid my bills when I was unemployed will provide for me now.*
  >
  > *The Lord who healed my body will heal my broken heart.*
  >
  > *The Lord who gave me courage to apologize will give me courage to make my presentation at work.*

- **Close your time by thanking God** for all He has done in you, through you, and for you. Ask Him to strengthen your God-confidence in specific ways this week as you engage the challenges you face.

- **Write down your declaration of confidence** on a sticky note or small card and either keep it with you or post it someplace where you will see it often. Allow it to shape how you view and respond to your everyday challenges. At the end of each day, briefly write down any insights or observations about your experiences.

Bring your notes and observations to the next group gathering. You'll have a chance to talk about what you learned at the beginning of the Session 3 discussion.

Closing Prayer

Close your time together with prayer.

Personal Study

Read and Learn

Read chapter 2 of *The Longing in Me.* Use the space below to note any insights or questions you want to bring to the next group session.

Study and Reflect

A girl will do almost anything to be protected.
The Longing in Me, page 24

1. In order to feel safe and protected, human beings need such assurances as predictability, stability, and freedom from fear. As you consider this season in your life, in which of the following area(s) would you say you are most aware of your need for safety and protection? Place a check mark next to your top two or three.

I am most aware of my need for . . .

☐ *Physiological safety* (food, clean water, clothing, shelter, etc.)

☐ *Physical wellness and security* (absence of illness/injury or other physical threat; adequate rest, healthy weight and fitness, etc.)

☐ *Job security* (the dignity of using skills and energy to serve and add value; the ability to generate income and provide for myself and my family, etc.)

☐ *Financial security* (ability to consistently pay bills, be debt-free, have an emergency fund, personal savings, insurance, retirement savings, etc.)

☐ *Emotional safety* (peace of mind, freedom from fear, healing for past wounds, etc.)

☐ *Aspirational safety* (ability and opportunity to grow personally, to achieve goals and dreams, to be strong and competent, etc.)

☐ *Relational safety* (ability to have meaningful, growing, trustworthy relationships with others)

☐ *Spiritual safety* (ability to have a meaningful, growing, trustworthy relationship with God)

☐ *Social safety* (a sense of belonging, value, and acceptance from those in my social circles)

☐ *Civil safety* (the expectation of being treated equally and fairly by systems of justice and social welfare)

☐ *"Future" security* (assurance about unknowns; that nothing bad will happen to me or my loved ones)

☐ *Other*: _____

_____

_____

_____

_____

For each of the items you checked, briefly identify what you imagine might happen if your fears are realized. For example: *If I don't have financial security, I am afraid I won't be able to pay medical bills or have enough money to live on when I retire. My whole life will become hard and uncertain.*

_____

_____

_____

If you don't challenge it in the name of the Lord, fear will occupy more and more territory of your heart and mind.

The Longing in Me, page 31

2. Questions 3 and 4 in the group discussion contrasted David's and Saul's responses to the threat of Goliath. Although the threat was the same, they reacted in radically different ways. David was mobilized by his confidence in God; Saul was immobilized by his fears. David saw the threat through a God-dominated imagination, and Saul saw the threat through a Goliath-dominated imagination.

Choose *one* of the fears you identified in the question 1 checklist. Overall, how would you assess your response to it? Circle the number on the continuum that best describes your answer.

1	2	3	4	5	6	7	8	9	10

Call Me Saul
I feel immobilized by
my fears.

Call Me David
I feel mobilized by my
confidence in God.

If you circled a number closer to the right (6 – 10), what practices, experiences, or relationships are helping you to have confidence in God? If you circled a number closer to the left (1 – 5), what makes it difficult for you to move beyond your fears right now?

_____

_____

_____

_____

One of the insights from David and Saul's story is that we always have a choice. No matter how big the threat we face, we have the freedom to choose our response. We can choose to be shaped by our fears, or we can choose to be shaped by our faith.

Overall, would you say you mostly feel free to choose your response to the fear you identified, or do you mostly feel trapped and unable to choose? Why?

_____

_____

_____

_____

In what ways is your response shaped by your fears? In what ways is it shaped by your faith?

_____

_____

_____

_____

> David was the only one who understood a life-altering truth:
> No matter how big the giant you face right now, God is big-
> ger. He is the protecting One.
>
> *The Longing in Me*, page 28

3. Even when we choose to be shaped by our faith — to trust that God is our protector — it can be hard to reconcile with the fact that we still experience harm, loss, and hardship. Although there is no easy answer, the Bible doesn't flinch from acknowledging both the certainty of suffering and the assurance of God's protection. John 16 records a compelling exchange between Jesus and His disciples that explores this very tension.

   Shortly before His arrest and crucifixion, Jesus is preparing His disciples for His death and the hardships and suffering they will soon face, some of them life-threatening. And He tells them not only what will happen to them but how they will fail Him — that they will be scattered and abandon Him, leaving Him alone when He needs them most. Moreover, He says He is about to leave them, and they will experience deep grief. It's a sobering litany of very bad news. But Jesus also gives His disciples assurances that throughout all of these devastating realities to come, they will know God's relentless care, provision, and presence:

   * The disciples will soon abandon Him, but Jesus' confidence in God's protection is unshaken: "Yet I am not alone because the Father is with me" (John 16:32).

   * Jesus will leave the disciples, but something better is coming: "It is best for you that I go away, because if I don't, the Advocate won't come. If I do go away, then I will send him to you.... When the Spirit of truth comes, he will guide you into all truth" (John 16:7, 13).

   * The disciples will experience loss; they will weep and mourn; but Jesus promises, "Your grief will suddenly turn to wonderful joy ... and no one can rob you of that joy" (John 16:20, 22).

Here is how Jesus then summarizes the reconciling truth in what appears to be an irreconcilable tension—that they will face suffering *and* that He is their protector:

> "I've told you all this so that trusting me, you will be unshakable and assured, deeply at peace. In this godless world you will continue to experience difficulties. But take heart! I've conquered the world." (John 16:33 MSG)

Take a moment to think back to David and Saul. In what ways does David's response to the threat of Goliath illustrate Jesus' summary statement?

_____

_____

_____

_____

How does Jesus' statement and the teaching in John 16 challenge you and/or encourage you about the fear you focused on in question 2?

_____

_____

_____

_____

Included in Jesus' assurances (listed above in bullet points) are at least three promises we can claim:

You are never alone. God is always with you.

You have an Advocate who will guide you into all truth.

Grief never has the last word. God always has the last word: joy.

Which of these promises resonates most with you right now? How might it strengthen your confidence in God's presence and protection?

_____

_____

_____

4. God's protection and deliverance are prominent themes of many psalms, including Psalm 27, in which David expresses his deep confidence that God will keep him safe. "Though an army besiege me," he writes, "my heart will not fear; though war break out against me, even then I will be confident" (verse 3 NIV). Read through the psalm slowly and prayerfully, allowing the words of David the giant slayer to fill you with peace and confidence. Then use the space below to write your own prayer. Ask God to be the stronghold of your life and to strengthen your confidence in His protection and care. Don't hesitate to share your fears, questions, and requests, asking Him for whatever you need to meet the challenges or uncertainties you face.

Longing for Control

Self-surrender has, of course, to be continually repeated.

C. E. B. Cranfield, *Romans*

Checking In (10 minutes)

A key part of getting to know God better is sharing your journey with others. Before watching the video, briefly check in with one another about your experiences since the last session. For example:

- Briefly share your experience of the Session 2 practice activity, "Write Your Spiritual Resumé." What did you learn or experience as you reflected on your life with God—what God has done in you, through you, and for you?

- In what ways, if any, did your declaration of confidence shape the way you responded to everyday challenges or strengthen your confidence in God?

- What insights did you discover in the personal study or in the chapter you read from *The Longing in Me*?

- How did the previous session impact your daily life or your relationship with God?

- What questions would you like to ask the other members of your group?

Video: Longing for Control (17 minutes)

Play the video segment for Session 3. As you watch, use the outline provided to follow along or to take additional notes on anything that stands out to you.

Notes

We must learn to let go and let God lead us.

_____

_____

_____

_____

_____

Control is a big issue for women.

There are choices we can make when those around us don't cooperate with our efforts to control. We can:

- Spiritualize the situation
- Punish the person
- Withdraw
- Give up our attempts at control and see what God will do

Story of Saul, David, Jonathan, and Ahimelek

Barbara Johnson story

"Be anxious for nothing, but in everything by prayer and supplication with thanksgiving let your requests be made known to God. And the peace of God, which surpasses all comprehension, will guard your hearts and your minds in Christ Jesus" (Philippians 4:6–7 NASB).

Giving thanks shifts everything inside of us. It's us saying to God, "I don't know how you'll do this, but you are God and you do all things well, and I trust you. I let go."

When we worship instead of worry, the peace of Christ will flood our hearts and minds.

David learned an important lesson about what happens when we attempt to control something that is better left in God's domain. The high tides will certainly come and wash us away, or a low tide will leave us exposed and unprotected. The good news is that redemption and forgiveness are not just possible but actually a promise!

Group Discussion (31 minutes)

Take a few minutes to talk about what you just watched.

1. What part of the teaching had the most impact on you?

Controlled and Controlling

2. Sheila described three ways we sometimes try to control others:

    We spiritualize the situation: *I'm upset because I don't believe this is what the Lord wants. I've prayed about this, and I don't have peace about it. It's God's will that . . .*

We punish the person: *It's fine if you want to do that, but I can't be part of it. If you're not interested in helping with my volunteer opportunity, I'm not interested in your party.*

We withdraw: *I won't yell and scream—I just won't talk at all. Until you realize what you did, I don't want to be around you. I'll be civil, but that's all you'll get from me from now on.*

- Take a moment on your own to consider your experiences on the receiving end of someone else's controlling behavior. The behavior might have been mild and subtle, blatant and aggressive, or somewhere in between. Once you identify an experience or two, share with the group which, if any, of the three categories of control (listed above) your experiences fall into. Then share not so much about what the other person did or said but how it affected you. For example, did you comply with or resist their efforts to control you? What was your emotional response? How did the controlling behavior influence your view of the other person or your relationship with them?

- Now take a moment on your own to consider your own controlling behaviors, perhaps focusing on something you did in the last day or two. Again, the behavior might have been mild and subtle, blatant and aggressive, or somewhere in between. Share your experience with the group, focusing less on the specifics of what you did and more on what was happening inside you when you did it. For example, what thoughts and emotions were you experiencing, and how did they shape your behavior? How did your behavior affect the other person or your relationship with them?

- Sheila pointed out that part of our need for control comes from legitimate desires; we want good things: peaceful lives, safety for our families, a fulfilling marriage, meaningful friendships. How would you describe the legitimate desire behind your controlling behaviors? What is the good thing you hoped to achieve for yourself or others? To what degree did you achieve it?

- What insights might your experience of engaging in controlling behavior provide about your experience with the person who tried to control you? Or how does being on the receiving end of controlling behavior help you to understand something about the impact of your own controlling behaviors?

Controlling What We Can, Surrendering What We Can't

Optional Activity: Saul, David, and Jonathan (10 minutes)

If time permits, read together the stories of Saul, David, and Jonathan recorded in 1 Samuel 18:1 – 16; 21:1 – 9; and 22:1 – 21 — each person reading aloud four or five verses at a time. As the passages are read, pay particular attention to how the three men responded when things didn't go their way, as well as any descriptions or clues about what motivated their behavior.

3. Sheila pointed out that when people don't cooperate with our efforts to control, we can either surrender ourselves and the situation to God or resort to manipulative or even destructive behaviors. All of these responses are evident in the stories she shared of Saul, David, and Jonathan.

   Saul began to feel threatened by David's success and popularity, and repeatedly tried to kill him. "What more can [David] get but the kingdom?" he thought (1 Samuel 18:8 NIV). After failing to kill David himself, Saul resorted to giving him dangerous military assignments in hopes David would be killed in battle. Over time, his jealousy and anger escalated into an all-consuming fear and hatred: "Saul was then afraid of David, for the LORD was with David and had turned away from Saul.... He remained David's enemy for the rest of his life" (1 Samuel 18:12, 29).

David initially surrendered control of his perilous situation to God. Even though he knew God had anointed him to be king, he didn't retaliate against Saul or try to sway others to his side. But when fear set in and he felt desperate to control an out-of-control situation, David lied to the priest Ahimelek to get what he wanted—bread and a weapon (see 1 Samuel 21:1–9). This turned out to be a disastrous choice that resulted in great loss of life. Though Ahimelek was innocent of treason, Saul ordered the slaughter of Ahimelek, his family, eighty-five priests, and all the residents of Nob, including their cattle, donkeys, and sheep (see 1 Samuel 22:18–19). The killings were Saul's decision, but David took responsibility for the deaths (see 1 Samuel 22:22).

Jonathan's response to the high-stakes drama that played out between Saul and David stands in stark contrast to their destructive and manipulative actions. Even though he was the rightful heir to Saul's throne, Jonathan recognized the hand of God on David, and he submitted to God's choice—not resentfully but with great love and devotion. He longed for the will of God more than he longed for his own rights or position. This brief but symbolically rich passage demonstrates Jonathan's heart:

> There was an immediate bond between them, for Jonathan loved David.... And Jonathan made a solemn pact with David, because he loved him as he loved himself. Jonathan sealed the pact by taking off his robe and giving it to David, together with his tunic, sword, bow, and belt. (1 Samuel 18:1, 3–4)

Jonathan's gifts to David symbolized his royal position and his military authority, both of which he willingly gave to David.

* Briefly identify any similarities you notice in the emotions and motives behind Saul's and David's controlling choices. What insights might these similarities provide about what fuels or escalates controlling behavior?

_____

_____

_____

- Using Saul as a reference, how would you characterize the person who is intent on control regardless of consequences or cost?

- Using Jonathan as a reference, how would you characterize the person who is intent on surrender to God regardless of consequences or cost?

- Like most of us, David alternated between seizing control (like Saul) and surrendering control to God (like Jonathan). In your own life, how have your experiences of seizing control on one occasion affected your desire or ability to surrender control to God on the next occasion?

4. Eventually David realized his mistake in trying to control things by deceiving Ahimelek. When he took his parents to Moab to keep them safe from Saul, he said to the king of Moab, "Please allow my father and mother to live here with you *until I know what God is going to do for me*" (1 Samuel 22:3, emphasis added). At this point, David's future was just as precarious as when he lied to Ahimelek, but he was through with trying to manipulate himself into safety. Instead, he surrendered control of his situation back to God and waited. This kind of surrender, what is sometimes referred to as "death to self," is a certain cure for controlling behavior. Author and pastor Dallas Willard defines this kind of surrender as "the willingness to trust the Kingdom of God where we are with what we are and what we're doing in a way that will allow that Kingdom to come into play."[6]

- How do you recognize the various components of Willard's definition in the lives of both David and Jonathan? How did their willingness to surrender to God enable the kingdom to come into play?

- In what small or large ways have you experienced the kind of surrender Willard describes? How did the kingdom come into play as a result? In other words, what did God do for you that you could not have done for yourself?

5. Sheila told the story of her friend Barbara Johnson who, like David, made some controlling decisions that led to damage she couldn't undo. She couldn't go back, but she could choose to move forward by living more wisely. She said that when you give your heartache and pain to God and trust Him with the outcome, you find freedom.

- Barbara was known for the phrase "Whatever, Lord!" She said it not in bitter resentment or because she'd given up, but because she believed three things: that God was good, that He loved her, and that she could trust Him with the timing. Which of these three things is hardest for you to believe when you have to wait for God? Share the reasons for your response.

- Barbara waited more than eleven years for restoration of the relationship with her estranged son. While she waited, she redeemed the time by channeling her desire to "do something" into ministering to other hurting parents. In your own life, how would you distinguish between doing something controlling and doing something to redeem the time, as Barbara did? What characterizes the key differences between the two?

Hearts Together

6. Spend a few moments reflecting on what you've learned and experienced together in this study so far.

   - How has learning more about longings overall impacted you or your relationship with God?

   - Since the first session, what shifts have you noticed in yourself in terms of how you relate to the group? For example, do you feel more or less guarded, understood, challenged, encouraged, connected, etc.?

   - What adjustments, if any, would you like to make to the Session 1 chart that would help other members of the group know how to be a good friend to you?

Individual Activity: What I Want to Remember (2 minutes)

Complete this activity on your own.

1. Briefly review the video outline and any notes you took.

2. In the space below, write down the most significant thing you gained in this session—from the teaching, activities, or discussions.

What I want to remember from this session . . .

_____

_____

_____

_____

_____

Practice: Let Go and Look for God

In the video, Sheila pointed out that our attempts at control often take one of three forms: we spiritualize the situation, we punish the person, or we withdraw. The practice this week is to let go of these and other attempts at control and to follow the example of David, who learned to wait "until I know what God is going to do for me" (1 Samuel 22:3).

*   ***Identify a relationship/situation in which you routinely struggle to let go of controlling thoughts and behaviors.*** It might be a relatively small, short-term situation or a larger and long-term situation. Use your journal or a notepad to briefly summarize the relationship/situation. If you find it helpful, use the following prompts:

    Who I want to control:

    What I want to control:

    When I want to control:

    Where I want to control:

    Why I want to control:

    How I want to control: (cont.)

- *Surrender yourself and your situation to God.* Author and pastor Adele Calhoun describes this process as replacing our attachment to self with "wholehearted attachment to and trust in God alone."* Allow this question to guide your prayer: "Lord, what do I need to let go of so that I can receive what You are going to do for me?" As best you are able, entrust yourself and anything you need to let go of to God. Ask for His help to wait until you see what He is going to do for you.

- *Look for God.* In our lives with God, waiting is not a time to do nothing. Instead, it is a time to be alert and active in what we already know God requires of us. "Wait for the LORD *and keep his way*," writes the psalmist (Psalm 37:34 ESV, emphasis added). We also wait with hope and expectation, believing that God is already active on our behalf (see Psalm 130:5). Whenever you engage the relationship/situation you have entrusted to God, focus your attention on waiting and looking for any signs of God at work, trusting that God is *always* at work, even when we can't see it.

- *Let it go, moment by moment.* Whenever you feel tempted to reassert control, ask yourself, "What does letting go and looking for God require of me in this moment?" Then do it. Allow letting go and looking for God to shape everything about your response — your demeanor, your body language, your words, your actions.

Throughout the week, use your journal or notepad to briefly note your experiences, challenges, and progress, as well as any signs you notice of God at work — in you and in your relationship/situation. Bring your notes to the next group gathering. You'll have a chance to talk about your experiences and observations at the beginning of the Session 4 discussion.

* Adele Calhoun, *Spiritual Disciplines Handbook: Practices That Transform Us* (Downers Grove, Ill.: InterVarsity Press, 2005), 95.

Closing Prayer

Close your time together with prayer.

SESSION THREE

Personal Study

Read and Learn

Read chapter 2 of *The Longing in Me*. Use the space below to note any insights or questions you want to bring to the next group session.

Study and Reflect

We long for peace but we often grab control because it makes us feel that we are doing something.

The Longing in Me, page 69

1. One of the challenges of dealing with controlling behavior is that while it may be easy to spot in other people, it's often hard to recognize in ourselves. Use the questions that follow to briefly assess the degree to which you might be engaging in controlling thoughts and behaviors. For each statement, circle the number on the continuum that best describes your response.

   a. I sometimes believe I will be happier if I can change someone else's undesirable behavior.

1	2	3	4	5	6	7	8	9	10
Not at all true of me.				Moderately true of me.				Completely true of me.	

   b. I have changed my opinion or behaviors in order to be accepted by someone or to manage their impression of me.

1	2	3	4	5	6	7	8	9	10
Not at all true of me.				Moderately true of me.				Completely true of me.	

   c. I often feel like I know better.

1	2	3	4	5	6	7	8	9	10
Not at all true of me.				Moderately true of me.				Completely true of me.	

   d. I have flattered or flirted with others to increase the odds of getting what I want from them.

1	2	3	4	5	6	7	8	9	10
Not at all true of me.				Moderately true of me.				Completely true of me.	

   e. I make it hard for people to say no to me.

1	2	3	4	5	6	7	8	9	10
Not at all true of me.				Moderately true of me.				Completely true of me.	

   f. I sometimes take on tasks or projects because I don't think anyone else will do it right.

1	2	3	4	5	6	7	8	9	10
Not at all true of me.				Moderately true of me.				Completely true of me.	

   g. I think ten steps ahead of everyone else, trying to anticipate what will happen so I am never taken off guard.

1	2	3	4	5	6	7	8	9	10
Not at all true of me.				Moderately true of me.				Completely true of me.	

h. I've been known to retaliate or punish people when things don't go my way.

1	2	3	4	5	6	7	8	9	10
Not at all true of me.				Moderately true of me.				Completely true of me.	

i. I find myself sitting in silent judgment of others if their behavior doesn't meet my expectations.

1	2	3	4	5	6	7	8	9	10
Not at all true of me.				Moderately true of me.				Completely true of me.	

j. I'm not satisfied when things are less than perfect—and I don't think others should be either.

1	2	3	4	5	6	7	8	9	10
Not at all true of me.				Moderately true of me.				Completely true of me.	

k. I've been described as pushy, stubborn, or manipulative.

1	2	3	4	5	6	7	8	9	10
Not at all true of me.				Moderately true of me.				Completely true of me.	

l. I collect "ammunition" I can use to get my way.

1	2	3	4	5	6	7	8	9	10
Not at all true of me.				Moderately true of me.				Completely true of me.	

m. I sometimes spiritualize a situation, using religious language or references to justify my personal preferences or to get things to go my way.

1	2	3	4	5	6	7	8	9	10
Not at all true of me.				Moderately true of me.				Completely true of me.	

n. I sometimes try to get what I want indirectly, by withholding approval, sulking, or exaggerating the positive or negative aspects of a situation.

1	2	3	4	5	6	7	8	9	10
Not at all true of me.				Moderately true of me.				Completely true of me.	

o. I sometimes think of people who don't behave in the way I want them to as "the enemy."

1	2	3	4	5	6	7	8	9	10
Not at all true of me.				Moderately true of me.				Completely true of me.	

Transfer the numbers you circled for each of the questions to the blank chart below. Add all the numbers and write the total in the space provided. Divide the total by 15 to determine your overall control score. (See example.)

EXAMPLE

My Responses		My Responses	
a.	3	a.	_____
b.	6	b.	_____
c.	2	c.	_____
d.	7	d.	_____
e.	4	e.	_____
f.	8	f.	_____
g.	10	g.	_____
h.	5	h.	_____
i.	6	i.	_____
j.	3	j.	_____
k.	7	k.	_____
l.	3	l.	_____
m.	5	m.	_____
n.	7	n.	_____
o.	6	o.	_____
Total	82	Total	_____

82 ÷ 15 = 5.4

My total   My control score

_____ ÷ 15 = _____

My total   My control score

Finally, plot your control score on the continuum below by marking it with an X. For example, an X between 5 and 6 would represent the 5.4 score from the example.

1	2	3	4	5	6	7	8	9	1 0

I rarely engage in controlling thoughts and behaviors.

I sometimes engage in controlling thoughts and behaviors.

I routinely engage in controlling thoughts and behaviors.

What is your initial response to your overall control score? For example, in what ways does it seem accurate or inaccurate to you?

Briefly review your responses to the fifteen questions and circle two or three you rated closest to 10. What relationships come to mind in connection with each of the statements you circled? Who recently has been on the receiving end of your controlling thoughts and behaviors?

2. In his letter to the church at Galatia, the apostle Paul contrasts life under the control of the Holy Spirit with life controlled by "what your sinful nature craves" (Galatians 5:16). *The Message* characterizes such a life as "trying to get your own way all the time," which is almost always the goal of controlling thoughts and behavior. The group session explored how this drive for control played out in the lives of King Saul and David, both of whom engaged in either aggressive control or subtle manipulation to get what they wanted (see the summary in question 3 of the group discussion). As you read the following passage from Galatians, underline any words or phrases that stand out to you, either in connection with King Saul and David or with your own controlling thoughts and behaviors.

> It is obvious what kind of life develops out of trying to get your own way all the time: repetitive, loveless, cheap sex; a stinking accumulation of mental and emotional garbage; frenzied and joyless grabs for happiness; trinket gods; magic-show religion; paranoid loneliness; cutthroat competition; all-consuming-yet-

never-satisfied wants; a brutal temper; an impotence to love or be loved; divided homes and divided lives; small-minded and lopsided pursuits; the vicious habit of depersonalizing everyone into a rival; uncontrolled and uncontrollable addictions; ugly parodies of community. I could go on. This isn't the first time I have warned you, you know. If you use your freedom this way, you will not inherit God's kingdom. (Galatians 5:19–21 MSG)

What insights does this passage provide about King Saul and David? In what ways do both men exemplify the "kind of a life that develops out of trying to get your own way all the time"?

In what ways do you relate to this passage, especially in connection with the controlling thoughts and behaviors you circled in question 1?

The group session explored how Jonathan's demeanor and behavior stood in stark contrast to that of both Saul and David. As you read the following passage that describes a life controlled by the Holy Spirit, underline any words or phrases that remind you of Jonathan or that highlight a characteristic you feel drawn to for any reason.

> But what happens when we live God's way? He brings gifts into our lives, much the same way that fruit appears in an orchard— things like affection for others, exuberance about life, serenity. We develop a willingness to stick with things, a sense of compassion in the heart, and a conviction that a basic holiness permeates things and people. We find ourselves involved in loyal commitments, not needing to force our way in life, able to marshal and direct our energies wisely. (Galatians 5:22–23 MSG)

What insights does this passage provide about Jonathan? In what ways does he exemplify living "God's way"?

_____

_____

_____

_____

_____

Which characteristics do you feel most drawn to or most in need of in order for you to let go of controlling behavior in the relationships you identified in question 1?

_____

_____

_____

_____

_____

_____

_____

In connection with the controlling thoughts and behaviors you circled in question 1, how would you say you are *forcing your way in life*? What do you think it might mean to *marshal and direct your energies wisely* instead?

_____

_____

_____

_____

_____

_____

_____

_____

_____

_____

Can you bring the thing you long to fix to God, give it to Him, and trust Him?

The Longing in Me, page 70

3. Read Psalm 25, a prayer of trust in which the psalmist affirms confidence in God but also expresses anxiety about the threats that surround him. The psalmist appeals to God for both guidance and forgiveness, demonstrating his utter dependence on God when he writes, "My eyes are always on the LORD" (Psalm 25:15). Read through the psalm slowly, receptive to how God might be inviting you to trust Him with the relationships and situations you can't control. Use the psalm as a reference in writing your own prayer, asking for the guidance you need in order to cease from forcing your way in life. Ask God to help you experience the freedom of letting go and trusting Him with what matters most to you.

Longing for Happiness

Everyone wants to be happy, to be blessed. Too many people are willfully refusing to pay attention to the one who wills our happiness and ignorantly supposing that the Christian way is a harder way to get what they want than doing it on their own. But they are wrong. God's ways and God's presence are where we experience the happiness that lasts. Do it the easy way.

Eugene Peterson, *A Long Obedience in the Same Direction*

Checking In (10 minutes)

A key part of getting to know God better is sharing your journey with others. Before watching the video, briefly check in with one another about your experiences since the last session. For example:

* Briefly share your experience of the Session 3 practice activity, "Let Go and Look for God." What did you learn or experience as you tried to surrender yourself and your situation to God? What did letting go require of you?

* In what ways, if any, did you experience God at work—in you and/or in your relationship/ situation?

* What insights did you discover in the personal study or in the chapter you read from *The Longing in Me*?

* How did the previous session impact your daily life or your relationship with God?

* What questions would you like to ask the other members of your group?

Video: Longing for Happiness (17 minutes)

Play the video segment for Session 4. As you watch, use the outline provided to follow along or to take additional notes on anything that stands out to you.

Notes

Cape Disappointment

Recap of David's story

He was about seventeen years old when Samuel anointed him.

The turning point came when he killed Goliath and went to King Saul's palace.

Then he had to run for his life. He fled Saul for thirteen years.

God told David to go to Hebron instead of going to Jerusalem or Judah. David stayed there for seven and a half years.

The elders of Israel came to David and made him king. It was twenty years from the promise to the fulfillment.

Everything flourished under his leadership, but prosperity wasn't enough for David. He made some bad choices.

David's strength was his passion, but it was also his Achilles' heel.

_____

_____

_____

When the time came for battle, David decided to send his general off to fight in his stead. If he had been performing what he was uniquely called and equipped to do, he never would have been on his roof one night watching another man's wife take a bath. David wasn't looking for evil; he just wasn't living where he should have been.

_____

_____

_____

The shocking thing was how easy it was for David to fall into sin. He saw no perceivable enemy, and that's when his real enemy showed up. The danger of personal isolation is one of the most tragic lessons from King David's life.

_____

_____

_____

Story of David and Bathsheba

David sent a servant to find out about the beautiful woman on the rooftop.

Every single one of us is capable of the most blatant sin given the right set of circumstances.

David had two choices: (1) own up to what he did, or (2) cover up the affair.

Panic is a poor foundation for making decisions. When David realized he couldn't bend Uriah to his will, he decided to kill him instead.

David got what he thought he needed to make him happy. He went after what he longed for: Bathsheba.

We wrongly think the truth will destroy us. It may hurt us in the short term, but it won't destroy us. That's the territory of the enemy.

_____

_____

_____

Miranda's story

She wanted to share her story and help other women get closer to God. She knew that would make her happy and give her life real purpose.

When she got up in front of all those women, she froze.

When God places a desire in our hearts, we need to trust Him with the "when." If God has something for us, He will never be too late or too early.

_____

_____

_____

The longings you have in the depth of your being will never be satisfied long-term by that one thing you think you need. True contentment and rest come from Christ. He alone can fill the deepest longings of your heart.

_____

_____

Group Discussion (31 minutes)

Take a few minutes to talk about what you just watched.

1. What part of the teaching had the most impact on you?

_____

_____

_____

_____

The Fog of Happiness

2. Sheila likened her pursuit of happiness to sailors searching for safe harbor in the fog. Before she married, she had idealistic and "foggy" ideas about what life would be like with her future husband. He was the one thing she felt she needed to be truly happy.

    *   If you could go back in time to your childhood, how do you imagine your childhood self might respond to the question "What do you need to be truly happy?" Use the phrase "if only" to state your response(s). For example:

        If only I had a talking Barbie, I would be truly happy.

        If only I could go to Disneyland, I would be truly happy.

        If only I could live at Grandma's, I would be truly happy.

        If only I could go swimming every day, I would be truly happy.

        If only I could have a puppy for Christmas, I would be truly happy.

_____

_____

_____

_____

- Now consider the same question, but this time from the perspective of your teenage self. Once again, use the phrase "if only" to state your response(s).

  _____

  _____

  _____

- How would you characterize the differences in your definition of happiness between your childhood and teen years?

  _____

  _____

  _____

- Overall, how would you describe what receiving or not receiving your "if only" taught you about happiness?

  _____

  _____

  _____

- The "one thing" we think will make us truly happy can change quite a bit over the course of our lives. How does thinking back on your childhood and teenage ideas of happiness influence your perspective on what you think you need to be truly happy in this season of your life?

  _____

  _____

  _____

Receiving God's Goodness, Trusting God's Timing

3. Up to this point in our journey with David, he has made some costly mistakes but remained a largely heroic figure and an example of what it means to be a person after God's own heart (see 1 Samuel 13:14). However, with the Bathsheba affair and its wicked

aftermath, David plummets from a role model to a cautionary tale. The deterioration in the condition of David's heart is revealed when God confronts him through the prophet Nathan:

> This is what the Lord, the God of Israel, says: "I anointed you king over Israel, and I delivered you from the hand of Saul. I gave your master's house to you, and your master's wives into your arms. I gave you all Israel and Judah. And if all this had been too little, I would have given you even more. Why did you despise the word of the Lord by doing what is evil in his eyes? You struck down Uriah the Hittite with the sword and took his wife to be your own. You killed him with the sword of the Ammonites. Now, therefore, the sword will never depart from your house, because you despised me and took the wife of Uriah the Hittite to be your own.... You have shown utter contempt for the Lord." (2 Samuel 12:7 – 10, 14 NIV).

• Before the Lord made any statements about David, he made several "I" statements about Himself, some of them repeatedly: *I anointed, I delivered, I gave, I gave, I would have given.* What do these statements reveal not only about God's character but, by implication, about the fundamental nature of David's offense? In other words, how had David's actions violated who God claimed to be in these statements?

_____

_____

_____

• Now consider God's "you" statements about David: *you despised, you did what is evil, you struck down, you took, you killed, you despised, you took, you showed utter contempt.* What stands out most to you about the contrasts between the statements God made about David and those God made about Himself?

_____

_____

_____

- The Lord detailed David's sinful actions, but the foundational charge He leveled against him wasn't his adultery with Bathsheba or even the murder of Uriah but his "utter contempt for the Lord." To better understand what this means, consider the following definitions of the word *contempt*:

    The state of mind of one who despises

    The feeling that a person is beneath consideration, worthless, or deserving scorn

    The attitude of regarding someone as inferior or base

    The feeling with which a person regards anything considered mean, vile, or worthless

    The word *utter* means "complete, entire, absolute." Drawing on all these definitions as a reference, how would you describe what it really means that David showed "utter contempt" for God? What was the condition of his mind and heart?

    _____

    _____

    _____

    _____

4. Tucked within the statements the Lord makes about Himself and about David in the 2 Samuel passage may be a clue that can help us explore not only what happened to David's heart but also what it means to find happiness and contentment in God alone. The Lord says of Himself twice, "I gave"; of David He says twice, "You took." Anything freely given is a gift, and there are only two things we can do with a gift—receive it or decline it. To *take* something, however small, is to assert power and ownership over it; and to take without permission is stealing. At some point along the way, David stopped receiving God's gifts, and perhaps eventually declined them outright. No longer a recipient of goodness from God, he developed a soul deficit, an emptiness he attempted to fill with what he could take for himself.

    - Take a moment to recall a time you gave someone an especially meaningful or significant gift—something you were certain would make this person very happy. Before giving the gift, what kind of response did you hope the recipient would have? What would have happened in your relationship if the recipient had not only failed to respond as you hoped but had actually declined the gift?

_____

_____

_____

- How does imagining the relational impact of declining a gift help you understand something about David's heart and his relationship with God?

  _____

  _____

  _____

- We sometimes forget that God created happiness, joy, and pleasure, and that God Himself is the "happiest, most joyful being in the universe."[7] As long as David had an intimate, receiving relationship with God, he was a man after God's own heart; when he stopped receiving and started taking, his heart grew deformed. What changes in your perspective if you think of your pursuit of happiness and joy less as an experience or a goal in itself and more as a means by which your heart is shaped one way or the other — *transformed* to be more like Jesus, or *deformed* over time as David's was?

  _____

  _____

  _____

5. At the end of the video, Sheila pointed out that when God places a desire in our hearts, we need to trust Him with the "when" — He is never too late or too early. For example, in David's life, twenty years passed from the time God anointed him until he actually became king, which meant divine gifts for David were hidden even within the waiting time between promise and fulfillment.

   - Based on what you know about David's life, how would you describe the gifts hidden within the decades he waited to become king? What might he have received from God in that time that he couldn't have received any other way?

     _____

     _____

- How might David's story have played out differently if he had declined the gifts hidden within his waiting time?

- Sheila shared the story of Miranda, who tried to accelerate the timing of her dream to become a speaker and experienced a painful failure as a result. In what ways, if any, do you relate to Miranda's experience? What sometimes makes it hard for you to believe God has gifts and a purpose for you even in the waiting time?

Hearts Together

6. Take a moment to touch base with one another about how you are doing in the group. Use one of the sentence starters below or your own statement to help the group learn more about how to be a good friend to you.

    I give you permission to challenge me more about . . .

    An area where I really need your help or sensitivity is . . .

    I feel more connected to the group when . . .

    Something I've learned about myself because of this group is . . .

Individual Activity: What I Want to Remember (2 minutes)

Complete this activity on your own.

1. Briefly review the outline and any notes you took.

2. In the space below, write down the most significant thing you gained in this session—from the teaching, activities, or discussions.

What I want to remember from this session . . .

_____

_____

_____

_____

Practice: Recognize, Receive, Give Thanks

One of the insights from David's story is about the connection between true happiness and the ability to continually recognize and receive God's gifts. When we stop recognizing and receiving in a love relationship with God, it won't be long until, like David, we start grabbing at lesser loves and end up on a path to failure and unhappiness. The practice for this week is to train the eye of your heart to routinely recognize and receive God's gifts by writing Him thank-you notes.

For the next five days, use your journal or a pad of paper (or actual stationery) to write daily thank-you notes to God. A meaningful thank-you note doesn't have to be long, but it does need to be authentic, specific, and heartfelt. That means you will need to pay attention throughout each day, looking for any sign of God's goodness and grace. You may want to keep a quick gratitude list to reflect on later when you sit down to write your thank-you note. If nothing on a given day inspires gratitude, or if you find getting started difficult, here are a few categories you might consider:

Relationships	Natural beauty
Food	Spiritual gifts or growth
Health or healing	God's strength, peace, or provision
Employment	Your five senses
Home	Opportunities/experiences
Education	Technology
Achievement or breakthrough	Good surprises
Reliable utilities (power, heat, clean water)	Talents/skills

Once you are ready to write your note, do so prayerfully and try not to rush. The purpose of the exercise is not just to express gratitude but to deepen your awareness of and connection with God. Here are some guidelines you can use for any thank-you note, including your thank-you notes to God:

- **Date it.** Gratitude is a function of memory, a reference to a specific gift or grace, received at a specific time and place. Dating a thank-you note and sending it promptly anchors it in time and may even become an ongoing source of gratitude if the note is reread at a later time.

- **Open with a greeting.** Every note begins with a greeting that reflects the writer's relationship with the recipient: *Dear Mom, Beloved, Dearest friend.* Open your note to God with a greeting that expresses something about your relationship with Him right now.

- **Express gratitude.** What are you thankful for? Avoid generalities and express your gratitude with specificity. For example, instead of "Thank You for the beauty of nature," a more specific expression might be, "Thank You for the Technicolor display of last night's sunset—the red, the gold, the deep purple. Wow!"

- *Revel in the details.* Add details that demonstrate not just your gratitude for the gift but your authentic enjoyment of it, the uniqueness of it, or how you anticipate the future benefit of it. For example, "I was so blown away by that sunset, I called my friend and told her to stop whatever she was doing and look out the window."

- *Affirm the connection between the gift and the giver.* The gift itself is important, but the relationship with the giver is what matters most. Acknowledge your love and appreciation for God, the giver of the gift. For example, "Thank You for using the beauty of the sunset to remind me again how much You love me."

- *Close with a word or phrase of love and respect.* This is sometimes referred to as one's "regards." For example, *Sincerely, Kind regards, With love, Your loving daughter.* Similar to the opening greeting, close your note to God with a phrase that affirms your relationship with Him right now, and then sign your name.

On the sixth day, reread your five thank-you notes. Use your journal or notepad to reflect on your experience of writing the notes. For example, what stands out to you about what you wrote—or what you didn't write? To what degree, if any, did the practice of writing the notes each day affect your ability to experience happiness and contentment in God?

Bring your written reflections to the next group gathering. Also bring along one of your thank-you notes if you'd feel comfortable sharing it with the group. You'll have a chance to talk about your experiences and observations at the beginning of the Session 5 discussion.

Closing Prayer

Close your time together with prayer.

Personal Study

Read and Learn

Read chapter 6 of *The Longing in Me.* Use the space below to note any insights or questions you want to bring to the next group session.

_____

_____

_____

_____

_____

_____

Study and Reflect

Perhaps you are in an "if only" place. You think, *If only I could have this one thing, be loved by this one person, be given this one opportunity, then I'd be happy.*

The Longing in Me, pages 103–104

1. In question 2 of the group discussion, you had a chance to discuss the "if only" things you believed would make you happy when you were a child, and then when you were a teenager. What comes to mind when you think about the "if only" desires in this season of your life? What do you need to be truly happy? Consider this question for each of the categories listed below.

    Finances

    If only ... _____

    _____

    _____

    Love life

    If only ... _____

    _____

    _____

    Family and friends

    If only ... _____

    _____

    _____

    Physical health or appearance

    If only ... _____

    _____

    _____

Work/daily responsibilities

If only . . .

Possessions

If only . . .

Experiences/opportunities

If only . . .

Lifestyle

If only . . .

Other

If only . . .

2. Briefly review the statements you wrote down in question 1. Using temperature as a gauge, how would you assess the overall intensity of your desire for happiness in this season of your life? Circle the number on the continuum that best describes your response.

1	2	3	4	5	6	7	8	9	10

COLD
I don't experience any
intensity in my desire
for happiness.

HOT
I experience a great
deal of intensity in my
desire for happiness.

Would you say the intensity of your desire for happiness right now is the highest it has ever been, the lowest, or somewhere in between?

_____

_____

_____

What would you say is the key factor that determined the number you circled?

_____

_____

_____

_____

Are you content with the number you circled, or do you wish it were lower or higher? Why?

_____

_____

_____

_____

_____

> True contentment and rest comes from Christ. He alone can
> fill the deepest longings of our hearts.
>
> *The Longing in Me*, page 104

3. The group session explored what happened in David's life when his pursuit of happiness went badly wrong (see 2 Samuel 11:1–26; 12:1–13). We may be tempted to think that perhaps David's desires were too intense and had become unmanageable, which then led him to make sinful choices. And while it's true that unbridled desire was a factor in David's downfall, author John Piper offers another perspective about how we can fail when it comes to the intensity of desire in our lives:

> Our mistake lies not in the intensity of our desire for happiness, but in the weakness of it.... All the evils in the world come not because our desires for happiness are too strong, but because they are so weak that we settle for fleeting pleasures that do not satisfy our deepest souls, but in the end destroy them.[8]

What insights might Piper's statement provide about what happened to David in his choice to have an affair with Bathsheba?

In what ways does Piper's statement challenge you in connection with the overall intensity of your desire for happiness (question 2)? For example, where might your desires be too weak, or in what areas of life might you be tempted to "settle"?

In what ways does Piper's statement encourage you in connection with the overall intensity of your desire for happiness? For example, how might the strength of your desires be evidence of spiritual health and vitality?

_____

_____

_____

_____

4. No matter how intense our desires for happiness or how God-honoring our desires may be, we will still have times in life when our longings go unfulfilled—the longed-for pregnancy never happens; the dreamed-of cure does not come; the hoped-for restoration fails. When the realization hits that we may never have that one thing we want so badly, we might find ourselves leaning toward one of two extremes—making our unfulfilled desire nothing or everything.

- *Nothing.* When we treat unfulfilled desire as nothing, we try to extinguish it, deny it, or lock it down somehow so the aching lack of what we want doesn't hurt so much.

- *Everything.* When unfulfilled desire is everything, it becomes the organizing principle of our life and identity. Even if we try to move beyond it, we feel stuck and can't let go. As a result, everything else in life is filtered through the lens of our lack.

In what ways, if any, do you recognize either of these tendencies—treating desires as nothing or everything—in connection with the desires you wrote down in question 1?

_____

_____

_____

The alternative to desire as nothing or everything is *enough.* We surrender the full intensity of our desire into God's care, trusting that God is good and God is enough—even when we lack the one thing we believe we need to be truly happy. We practice waiting in contentment (see Philippians 4:12–13). We trust that if our hands and hearts are open to receive from God, He will give us good gifts.

Briefly review your responses to question 1. Choose one of the desires you wrote down to focus on. What thoughts or emotions are you aware of when you consider surrendering this desire into God's care?

How would you describe the spiritual longing behind this desire? For example, in what ways might it represent something you long for in your relationship with God?

5. Read Psalm 37:1–9, a wisdom psalm, which includes both commands and promises about leading a God-honoring and happy life. "Take delight in the LORD," comes the command, which is then immediately followed by a promise, "and he will give you your heart's desires" (Psalm 37:4). As you read, invite God to speak to you, to help you receive both the commands and the promises as His words of loving counsel for you. Allow your prayer to be your response to what you hear.

Longing for God's Grace

If I care to listen, I hear a loud whisper from the gospel that
I did not get what I deserved. I deserved punishment and
got forgiveness. I deserved wrath and got love. I deserved
debtor's prison and got instead a clean credit history. I
deserved stern lectures and crawl-on-your-knees repentance;
I got a banquet — Babette's feast — spread for me.

Philip Yancey, *What's So Amazing about Grace?*

Checking In (10 minutes)

A key part of getting to know God better is sharing your journey with others. Before watching the video, briefly check in with each other about your experiences since the last session. For example:

- Briefly share your experience of the Session 4 practice activity, "Recognize, Receive, Give Thanks." What did you learn or experience as you trained the eye of your heart to recognize and receive God's gifts each day? How did this practice affect your ability to experience happiness and contentment in God?

- If you feel comfortable sharing it with the group, read one of your thank-you notes to God. In what ways, if any, did writing a formal thank-you note help you recognize and receive God's gifts?

- What insights did you discover in the personal study or in the chapter you read from *The Longing in Me*?

- How did the previous session impact your daily life or your relationship with God?

- What questions would you like to ask the other members of your group?

Video: Longing for God's Grace (18 minutes)

Play the video segment for Session 5. As you watch, use the outline provided to follow along or to take additional notes on anything that stands out to you.

Notes

Life is not a spectator sport. It is to be lived in vulnerability and truth and community.

I have no rights as a believer. I am a sinner saved by grace, called to live a surrendered life.

Sometimes God will take you to a dark, confining place before you can be set free by seeing the light. I'm talking about the light of reality and accepting the consequences of how your actions impact those around you. If you are a person who loves God and you want to live a godly life, unconfessed sin is going to tear you up inside.

Nathan rebukes David: "There were two men in a certain town. One was rich, and one was poor. The rich man owned a great many sheep and cattle. The poor man owned nothing but one little lamb he had bought. He raised that little lamb, and it grew up with his children. It ate from the man's own plate and drank from his cup. He cuddled it in his arms like a baby daughter. One day a guest arrived at the home of the rich man. But instead of killing an animal from his own flock or herd, he took the poor man's lamb and killed it and prepared it for his guest" (2 Samuel 12:1–4). David proclaims a harsh sentence on the thief and even says he deserves to die, not knowing he's passing sentence on himself.

It is the mercy of God that lets us feel the impact of our sin. Until we fully understand the weight of our sin, we can't truly celebrate the beauty of our costly redemption through God's grace.

David's heart had become hardened. The same is true of us when we hold on to sin. We become judgmental of others. It's only when we have tasted grace that we can share it with another sinner.

The consequences of David's sin: "The sword shall never depart from your house" (2 Samuel 12:10 ESV). David's response: "I have sinned against the Lord" (2 Samuel 12:13 ESV).

When faced with his sin, Saul tried to justify his actions and even attempted to spiritualize his disobedience. Samuel's response to Saul: "What is more pleasing to the Lord: your burnt offerings and sacrifices or your obedience to his voice?" (1 Samuel 15:22). Solomon would later write, "People who conceal their sins will not prosper, but if they confess and turn from them, they will receive mercy" (Proverbs 28:13).

Beside the Bonnie Brier Bush, the story of Flora and her father

God is so much bigger than your past. He is so much more merciful than your sin. He is so much stronger than your weakest moment. His plans for you are so much greater than your failures. He is for you—always for you. When you've been shown that kind of grace, you can't wait to share it with others.

Group Discussion (30 minutes)

Take a few minutes to talk about what you just watched.

1. What part of the teaching had the most impact on you?

We All Need Grace

2. Sheila described how she gave her life to Christ as a young girl, never rebelled, and spent two decades in ministry without really comprehending her need for grace. And she had misunderstandings about grace. She thought grace was for people who committed obvious sins or who had big problems. "I was just a scared little good girl," she said. "Why did I need grace?"

   • What kind of misunderstandings do you think the Christians you know commonly have about grace?

   • How would you describe your earliest understanding of who God's grace is for? For example, like Sheila, did you start out thinking grace is mostly for people who commit obvious sins or have big problems? Or did you have a different understanding of who needed grace?

The Light of Reality

3. David came face-to-face with the depth of his need for grace when confronted by the prophet Nathan. Sheila pointed out that several months had passed without David giving any observable indication of guilt or remorse for what he'd done. Although the hardened condition of David's heart may have been hidden from most, it was no secret to God's prophet. Nathan somehow knew that a direct confrontation would never penetrate the walls of David's heavily fortified heart. Author Eugene Peterson describes the condition of a heart like David's this way:

> The kingdom of self is heavily defended territory. . . . Most sin, far from being a mere lapse of morals or a weak will, is an energetically and expensively erected defense against God. Direct assault in an openly declared war on the god-self is extraordinarily ineffective. Hitting sin head-on is like hitting a nail with a hammer; it only drives it deeper.[9]

And so the prophet wisely chooses an indirect approach, which enables David to experience what Sheila described as his own "light of reality."

- How do you imagine things might have gone if Nathan had started by accusing David directly?

- Nathan chose the approach he did at least in part because he wanted David to experience the impact of his sin. Why was this important? How might it have affected David's ability to experience grace if he had acknowledged his guilt but without really experiencing the impact of his sin?

- Peterson characterizes most sin as an "energetically and expensively erected defense against God." (For an additional description of this kind of intentional resistance to God, see Zechariah 7:11–12.) Why might David, or anyone else, need such a defense?

- How do you respond to the idea that, most of the time, confronting sin directly only drives it deeper? Under what circumstances might each approach—direct and indirect—be effective in confronting sin?

- Overall, which approach has been most effective in helping you to experience your own "light of reality"—and then to experience grace?

4. David's response when confronted was an unadorned confession: "I have sinned against the LORD" (2 Samuel 12:13 ESV). Sheila compared David's response with that of King Saul when confronted by the prophet Samuel. In contrast to David, Saul not only tried to justify his actions and shift the blame for what he did, he even spiritualized his disobedience. Samuel's rebuke was swift:

> What is more pleasing to the LORD: your burnt offerings and sacrifices or your obedience to his voice? Listen! Obedience is better than sacrifice, and submission is better than offering the fat of rams. Rebellion is as sinful as witchcraft, and stubbornness as bad as worshiping idols. (1 Samuel 15:22–23)

Samuel began with a question and then used a series of comparisons to cut through the fog of Saul's spiritualized justifications and self-deception. First, he compared two good things to demonstrate what was better; then he compared two sins to point out that they were equally sinful. By both sets of comparison, Saul failed.

• God's prophets were effective not just because there was divine truth in the words they spoke but also because there was wisdom in how they engaged the human heart. How would you characterize the wisdom of Samuel's approach to Saul? For example, why might he have used a question rather than an accusation as a starting point? How did his comparisons shine the light of reality on Saul's self-deception?

_____

_____

_____

• It may be that the psalmist had Saul in mind when writing these lines of Psalm 40:

> In sacrifice and offering you have not delighted, but you have given me an open ear. Burnt offering and sin offering you have not required. Then I said, "Behold, I have come; in the scroll of the book it is written of me: I delight to do your will, O my God; your law is within my heart." (Psalm 40:6–8 ESV)

For additional insights, read the passage again from _The Message_:

> Doing something for you, bringing something to you — that's not what you're after. Being religious, acting pious — that's not what you're asking for. You've opened my ears so I can listen. So I answered, "I'm coming. I read in your letter what you wrote about me, and I'm coming to the party you're throwing for me." That's when God's Word entered my life, became part of my very being. (Psalm 40:6–8 MSG)

Using this and the 1 Samuel 15 passage as references, how would you characterize the heart that embraces grace versus the heart that refuses it?

_____

_____

_____

_____

5. At the end of the video, Sheila engaged in some Samuel-like comparisons when she said, "God is so much bigger than your past. He is so much more merciful than your sin. He is so much stronger than your weakest moment. His plans for you are so much greater than your failures. He is for you. Always for you!"

    •   Which of Sheila's comparisons do you resonate with most in this season of your life? If you feel comfortable, share the reasons for your response.

    _____

    _____

    _____

    •   How would you describe what it means that God is for us—that God is for you?

    _____

    _____

    _____

Hearts Together

6. At the end of each session, you've had the opportunity to spend some time talking about your connections within the group, and especially about how to be good friends to one another.

    •   What are your observations about this portion of the discussion? For example, what, if any, differences do you notice in yourself and in the group when you are talking about yourself in relationship to the group rather than about the content of the study, etc.?

    _____

    _____

    _____

    •   Do you tend to look forward to this portion of the discussion, or do you find yourself wishing you could avoid it? Why?

    _____

    _____

    _____

Individual Activity: What I Want to Remember (2 minutes)

Complete this activity on your own.

1. Briefly review the outline and any notes you took.

2. In the space below, write down the most significant thing you gained in this session — from the teaching, activities, or discussions.

What I want to remember from this session . . .

<hr />
<hr />
<hr />
<hr />

Practice: Embrace Grace

David spent many months carrying the burden of a hardened heart. Although we don't see much evidence of it in the 2 Samuel 11 – 12 account, we get a glimpse of the toll it took on him in these lines from Psalm 32: "When I refused to confess my sin, my body wasted away, and I groaned all day long. . . . My strength evaporated like water in the summer heat" (Psalm 32:3 – 4). When Nathan confronted him, David could have chosen Saul's approach and persisted in defending himself to God. Instead, he chose to confess his sin and embrace grace.

The practice this week is to set aside time in your calendar to listen for God's voice through prayerful reflection and to embrace grace through confession.

- Set aside twenty to thirty minutes to reflect and pray. If possible, settle into a quiet place where you won't be interrupted. Begin with a minute or two of prayerful silence, inviting God to speak to you and asking for ears to hear and respond to what God might say.

- Read Psalm 32, a psalm of David that celebrates God's forgiveness and grace. Receive the words of the psalm as God's words for you — words of counsel, promise, assurance, and steadfast love. The assurance of God's unfailing love and grace are the foundation for confession.

• In God's loving presence, consider the ways in which you may have closed your ears to God's voice or engaged in what Eugene Peterson described as an "energetically and expensively erected defense against God." Your defense might concern habits of thought or behavior, relationships, or circumstances. If you find it helpful, reflect on this question: *What is it I am trying very hard not to know about myself or my actions in this regard?*

• With specificity, acknowledge your guilt—the wrong you have done or the good you have left undone. Express your regret and sorrow, asking for God's strength to make things right, to apologize, or to make restitution where appropriate. Ask God to guard your heart and to help you make the changes you need to make to avoid repeating these failures in the future.

• Receive God's forgiveness and grace. You may wish to reread Psalm 32, which invites all who embrace grace to "Rejoice in the LORD and be glad.... Shout for joy, all you whose hearts are pure!" (Psalm 32:11). Thank God and praise Him for clearing you of guilt and embracing you with grace.

Use your journal or a notepad to briefly reflect on your experience of confession and embracing grace. Bring your written reflections to the next group gathering. You'll have a chance to talk about your experiences and observations at the beginning of the Session 6 discussion.

Closing Prayer

Close your time together with prayer.

Get a Head Start on the Discussion for Session 6

As part of the group discussion for Session 6, you'll have an opportunity to talk about what you've learned and experienced together throughout *The Longing in Me* study. Between now and your next meeting, take a few moments to review the previous sessions and identify the teaching, discussions, or practices that stand out most to you. Use the worksheet on the following pages to briefly summarize the highlights of what you've learned and experienced.

Head Start Worksheet

Take a few moments to reflect on what you've learned and experienced throughout *The Longing in Me* study. You may want to review notes from the video teaching, what you wrote down for "What I Want to Remember" at the end of each group session, observations from weekly practice notes, and responses in the personal studies. Here are some questions you might consider as part of your review:

• What insights did I gain from this session?

• What was the most important thing I learned about myself in this session?

• How did I experience God's presence or leading related to this session?

• How did this session impact my relationships with the other people in the group?

Use the spaces provided below and on the next page to briefly summarize what you've learned and experienced for each session.

Session 1: Longing to Be Chosen

Session 2: Longing to Be Protected

Session 3: Longing for Control

Session 4: Longing for Happiness

Session 5: Longing for God's Grace

Personal Study

Read and Learn

Read chapter 7 of *The Longing in Me.* Use the space below to note any insights or questions you want to bring to the next group session.

Study and Reflect

Understanding grace is the work of God in our lives, and we
each walk our own journey to understanding it.
The Longing in Me, page 147

1. In the group session video, Sheila said it wasn't until she was at the lowest point in her life that she began to understand grace. How would you describe the beginning of your journey to understand grace—the point at which you knew grace was for you and you needed it? Check the statement on the next page that best describes your response.

My journey to understanding grace began when . . .

☐ I was a child or adolescent and learned about the plan of salvation in church.

☐ I heard about Jesus from a friend and wanted what s/he had.

☐ I was searching for meaning and purpose.

☐ I was exhausted from trying to earn God's love and acceptance.

☐ I had failed badly and was desperate for help and forgiveness.

☐ I experienced significant hardship, trauma, or loss and needed hope.

☐ I felt overwhelmed by God's goodness and generosity.

☐ I hit rock bottom in a personal struggle.

☐ Other: _____

> Forgiveness is a beautiful, costly gift offered when we've messed up, but grace is what we need for the long walk home toward wholeness.
>
> *The Longing in Me*, page 131

2. Wherever we begin with our understanding of grace, once we experience it, we soon discover that our need for grace never ends. In fact, we need more and more grace as we grow. In the second New Testament letter that bears his name, the apostle Peter writes as a pastor and shepherd, encouraging his readers to pursue their growth and maturity in Christ. As part of the letter's opening and closing remarks, Peter highlights the ongoing necessity of grace:

> May God give you more and more grace and peace. (2 Peter 1:2)

> You must grow in the grace and knowledge of our Lord and Savior Jesus Christ. (2 Peter 3:18)

In both statements, Peter makes it clear that grace is a grow thing—and the expectation is that our reliance on it will increase. The Greek word Peter uses for "grow" is *auxanō* (owx-an-o). It means to "increase in quantity or quality," and was used to describe the process of growth in plant life.[10]

For most plants, growth includes both hidden and observable growth. The hidden growth happens below ground as the plant sinks roots deep into the soil; the observable growth happens above ground as the plant produces some form of greenery, foliage, flowers, fruit, or seeds. Using the process of plant growth as a reference, how would you characterize the condition of grace in your life right now?

3. Author and pastor Dallas Willard defines grace as "God acting in our life to bring about, and enable us to do, what we cannot do on our own."[11] That includes the grace of forgiveness and reconciliation when we surrender our lives to Christ, but it doesn't stop there. He describes how grace functions in the life of the believer this way:

> To "grow in grace" means to utilize more and more grace to live by, until everything we do is assisted by grace. Then, whatever we do in word or deed will all be done in the name of the Lord Jesus (Colossians 3:17). The greatest saints are not those who need less grace, but those who consume the most grace, who indeed are most in need of grace—those who are saturated by grace in every dimension of their being. Grace to them is like breath.[12]

How does Willard's definition of grace help you understand your need for grace in this season of your life? For example, in what relationships, circumstances, or struggles are you most aware of your need for God to bring about or enable you to do something you cannot do on your own?

If we associate grace primarily with salvation or our need for forgiveness when we sin, we might find ourselves rationing our reliance on grace, thinking that growth in Christ means we should need grace less. Or we might even feel as though repeatedly accessing grace somehow exhausts God's patience or our limited lifetime allotment of grace. In what ways, if any, might you be rationing your access to grace or perhaps even avoiding the grace you need right now?

4. Read Psalm 145, a psalm of David that praises God for His abundant goodness. One biblical scholar describes this psalm as a hymn and gives it the title "Tell of His Might, Sing of His Grace!"[13] As you read, note the evidence of how pervasive God's grace and goodness are by the psalmist's repeated use of the word *all*. Wherever the *all* refers to persons, personalize the statement with *me* or *I*. For example, "The Lord is good to *all*" becomes "The Lord is good to *me*," and "so that *all people* may know of your mighty acts" becomes "so that *I* may know of your mighty acts" (Psalm 145:9, 12 NIV, emphasis added). Allow the psalm to be a means of God's grace to you, offering you the assurance of God's compassion and loving faithfulness especially and specifically for you. In response, write a prayer in which you receive the grace God offers, ask for the ongoing grace you need, and thank God for His abundant goodness to you.

Longing for God Alone

God wishes to be seen, and he wishes to be sought, and

he wishes to be expected, and he wishes to be trusted.

Julian of Norwich, *Showings*

Checking In (10 minutes)

A key part of getting to know God better is sharing your journey with others. Before watching the video, briefly check in with each other about your experiences since the last session. For example:

- Briefly share your experience of the Session 5 practice activity, "Embrace Grace." What was it like to reflect on your life and to practice confession? To receive and celebrate forgiveness?

- What insights did you discover in the personal study or in the chapter you read from *The Longing in Me*?

- How did the previous session impact your daily life or your relationship with God?

- What questions would you like to ask the other members of your group?

Video: Longing for God Alone (21 minutes)

Play the video segment for Session 6. As you watch, use the outline provided to follow along or to take additional notes on anything that stands out to you.

Notes

I see a common thread running through our stories—the longing and the ache for more of God.

_____

_____

_____

Unless we have been radicalized by the cross, we will inevitably be radicalized by something else, whether it's money or relationships, or status, or even our own brand of holiness. Only a vision of the greatness of God causes us to relinquish our pursuit of things and, instead, to kneel at his feet.

_____

_____

_____

As we've turned through the pages of David's life, we've seen sin but we've also seen humility, worship, trust, hope, repentance, strength, and love. Perhaps the greatest gift of David's life to us is his absolute trust in the goodness and mercy of God, no matter what raged around him. His story reminds us that it's not how you start in life that matters, but how you finish it.

Story of Absalom, Tamar, and Amnon

David models for us how to live: we worship God and we long for Him alone. When nothing else makes sense, we thank God for who He is and how He loves us. We cry out to the heavens and declare that the Lord watches over us. He is our shield; He is our defender.

David refused to fight for power. His bottom line was, *If God is through with me, then I am through. If He's not, then no matter what anyone tries to do, God will vindicate me.*

More than God's power, David desired God's will.

How do we live through tough times? What do you do when the road ahead is a long one? How do we look to God alone as our source of strength? We worship. Even when there is no light on the path, or dawn on the horizon, we worship God. We join with David and say, "I lay down and slept, yet I woke up in safety, for the Lord was watching over me" (Psalm 3:5).

I believe we search for God with all our longings. Every longing we try to satisfy apart from God will always fall short because, as Augustine once wrote, our hearts are restless until they rest in thee.

Just as God in Christ pursued us through the mud, the mire, the beatings, and up that bloody path to the cross, He now calls us to pursue Him. He promises that if we seek Him, we will find Him.

If you've made poor choices in your life, I urge you not to hide them. Instead, allow the piercing light of God's love to reveal the sin and heal your heart. Your story is one of the greatest gifts you can give to another person.

Group Discussion (27 minutes)

Take a few minutes to talk about what you just watched.

1. What part of the teaching had the most impact on you?

Longing for Home

2. Sheila likened the longing we have for God to a longing for home. To long for home or to feel homesick is to be preoccupied with thoughts of home and all the things we miss. According to clinical psychologist Christopher Thurber, homesickness is evidence of what we love and feel attached to:

> [We get homesick because] there are things that we love—it's the byproduct of the strength of our attachment. If there were nothing in the world we were attached to, then we wouldn't miss [it] when we're away.[14]

Thurber goes on to explain that what we really miss when we are homesick is not so much our home or even a familiar environment, but the love, security, and protection we tend to associate with those things.

- Briefly describe the last time you felt homesick. For example, it may have been when you were a child at summer camp or a student away at college, or perhaps it was more recently when travel took you away from home. How did homesickness affect you? What specifically did you miss and long for most?

_____

_____

_____

- Using your experience of homesickness as a reference, how would you characterize what it means to long for God, to be homesick for God?

_____

_____

_____

- Sheila said that the common thread she sees in the women she's met is a longing and ache for more of God. When do you tend to be most aware of your longing for God? Try to focus not just on your desire for something you need from God but on your longing for God's person—for intimacy and connection with God.

_____

_____

_____

3. In *The Return of the Prodigal Son*, author Henri Nouwen describes his own longing for God, and how he struggled "to find God, to know God, to love God." He did everything he knew he was supposed to do—he faithfully prayed, read Scripture, served others, and did his best to avoid temptations. Even when he failed and felt close to despair, he kept trying. His breakthrough came when he began to understand something about the father in the story of the prodigal son (see Luke 15:11–32). He writes:

Now I wonder whether I have sufficiently realized that during all this time God has been trying to find me, to know me, and to love me. The question is not "How am I to find God?" but "How am I to let myself be found by him?" The question is not "How am I to know God?" but "How am I to let myself be known by God?" And, finally, the question is not "How am I to love God?" but "How am I to let myself be loved by God?" God is looking into the distance for me, trying to find me, and longing to bring me home. . . . I am beginning now to see how radically the character of my spiritual journey will change when I no longer think of God as hiding out and making it as difficult as possible for me to find him, but, instead, as the one who is looking for me while I am doing the hiding.[15]

- In what ways, if any, do you relate to Nouwen's struggle? How have you tried but felt dissatisfied in your efforts to find, know, and love God? Or to what degree have you felt that God is somehow making it as difficult as possible for you to find Him?

- Nouwen finds his breakthrough not so much in answers but in reframing his questions around God's initiative rather than his own. God always takes the initiative; God always loves first (see 1 John 4:19). Our task is not to initiate but to respond to God's initiative. How does this switch in perspective challenge you in connection with your longings for God? How does it encourage you?

- Which of Nouwen's three questions do you feel most drawn to: *How am I to let myself be found by God? How am I to let myself be known by God? How am I to let myself be loved by God?* Share the reasons for your response.

Lessons from David

4. Perhaps the times we are most aware of our deep longing for God are the times we are walking a long, hard road. It might be that we are in a season of suffering brought on through no fault of our own; or, as in the case of David, it might be that we are suffering through the long-term consequences of our own sin and failure.

   Throughout this study, we've witnessed many things in David's story: strength, confidence, surrender, humility, hope, worship, sin, and repentance. Sheila pointed out that perhaps David's greatest gift to us is how he demonstrated absolute trust in the goodness and mercy of God, no matter his circumstances. Even in the aftermath of Absalom's betrayal, when both his life and his kingdom were at stake, David desired God's will more than he desired God's power.

   - How does longing for God's will more than longing for God's power demonstrate David's longing for God? How would you characterize the key differences between the two desires?

   - Read aloud Psalm 3, the psalm David wrote when he fled from his son Absalom. Based on the psalm, how would you say David lived out his longing for God when he was in a hard place? In other words, how did he allow himself to be found by God, to be known by God, or to be loved by God?

- Consider for a moment the things that constitute your life and your kingdom—everything that matters most to you. If these things were at stake, how might you long for God's power? What shifts in you when you consider what it might mean to long more for God's will?

5. Sheila said that when nothing else in life makes sense, David provides a model for how we are to live. No matter our situation, the one thing we can always do is worship. We shift our focus from longing for God's power to change our circumstances to longing for God alone. We praise and thank God for who He is and how He loves us. This is what it means to be a person after God's own heart.

   In this season of your life, how do you sense God may be inviting you to worship—to shift your focus from longing for God's power to longing for God alone?

Hearts Together

6. Take a few moments to discuss what you've learned together throughout *The Longing in Me* study.

   - What would you say is the most important thing you learned or experienced through your study and sharing together?

   - How has what you've learned impacted you, or how have you recognized God at work in your life through the study?

   - How have you recognized God's work among you in the group?

Individual Activity: What I Want to Remember (2 minutes)

Complete this activity on your own.

1. Briefly review the outline and any notes you took.

2. In the space below, write down the most significant thing you gained in this session — from the teaching, activities, or discussions.

What I want to remember from this session . . .

_____

_____

_____

_____

Practice: Pursue Your Longing for God

The practice for this week is to pursue your longing for God by responding to God's initiative — all the ways God has and continues to demonstrate His love and His longing for you.

- Set aside fifteen to twenty minutes to spend time alone with God. If possible, settle into a quiet place where you won't be interrupted. Begin with a minute or two of prayerful silence, inviting God to speak to you.

- One at a time, prayerfully reflect on each of the following questions:

  Lord, how can I let myself be found by you?

  Lord, how can I let myself be known by you?

  Lord, how can I let myself be loved by you?

  If you find it helpful, use your journal or a notepad to write down whatever comes to mind as you pray and listen for God's leading. (cont.)

- Out of your prayer, identify one area of life in which you are longing for a demonstration of God's power. For example, it might be a challenging circumstance, a personal struggle, or a difficult relationship. Allow this to be the focus of pursuing your longing for God this week.

- As best you are able, surrender your situation to God, asking God to make your longing for His will greater than your longing for His power. Acknowledge your concerns and questions, and ask God for whatever it is you need from Him.

- Close your time of prayer with worship, praising and thanking God for who He is and for how He loves you.

- As you engage your situation throughout the week, pursue your longing for God by continually praying through one or more of the three questions and adding "right now." For example, *Lord, how can I let myself be loved by you right now?* Allow your longing for God and for God's will to shape everything about how you respond — your demeanor, your body language, your words, your actions.

- At the end of each day, briefly write down any insights or observations about your experiences.

If your group is ongoing, allow time at your next gathering to talk about your experience of pursuing your longing for God. If this is your last group meeting, consider sharing your experiences with a friend or another member of the group one-on-one.

Closing Prayer

Close your time together with prayer.

Personal Study

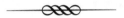

Read and Learn

Read chapter 10 of *The Longing in Me*. Use the space below to note any insights or questions you want to bring to the next group session.

_____

_____

_____

_____

_____

Study and Reflect

I believe we search for God with all our longings and all our lusts.

The Longing in Me, page 157

1. In the group session video, Sheila described how we sometimes try to meet our longings for God with other things. "The woman who has a hundred pairs of shoes in her closet is longing for more than foot fashion," she said. "The one who reaches for another drink is longing for more than just an alcohol-induced coma."

As you reflect on your own life, how have your longings—what you yearn for or crave—tended to express themselves? Place a check mark next to all that apply.

I have longed for . . .

☐ *Substances* (food, alcohol, tobacco, drugs, pornography, etc.)

☐ *Activities or experiences* (shopping, sex, exercise, Internet surfing, risky behavior, travel, extreme sports, gambling, etc.)

☐ *Achievements or recognition* (job promotion, grades, appearance, awards, sports or fitness, followers on social media, etc.)

☐ *Relationships* (romance, friendships, children, popularity, social media engagement, etc.)

☐ *Possessions* (gadgets, property/homes, shoes/clothes, jewelry, collections, etc.)

☐ *Other:* _____

In what ways, if any, has pursuing these longings provided you with something like a security blanket—a sense of belonging, of feeling comforted, or of being secure and cared for?

_____

_____

_____

_____

In what ways, if any, has pursuing these longings left you feeling "less than"—less than belonging, less than comforted, less than secure and cared for?

_____

_____

_____

_____

_____

If it's true that we search for God with all our longings, what insights do your longings provide about what you most need and long for from God?

_____

_____

_____

_____

> Jesus has proven Himself to me countless times. My longing
> has been redirected to Him, and He has filled me.
>
> *The Longing in Me*, page 171

2. Throughout this study, we've followed the life of David—from his obscurity as a no-account little brother and teenage shepherd, to his renown as a giant slayer and mighty king of Israel. Although he made grievous and costly mistakes, they aren't what we remember most about David or even what was most important about David. The most important thing about David was his longing and passion for God—it's what empowered his every accomplishment and what redeemed his every failure. It's why we know him to this day—sins and all—as a man after God's own heart (see Acts 13:22).

   If you long for the same to be true about you—that you are a woman after God's own heart—sooner or later you must come to terms with your longing for God. Author Ruth Haley Barton describes why this matters so much:

   > Your desire for more of God than you have right now, your longing for love, your need for deeper levels of spiritual transformation than you have experienced so far is the truest thing about you. You might think that your woundedness or your sinfulness is the truest thing about you or that your giftedness or your personality type or your job title or your identity as husband or wife, mother or father, somehow defines you. But in reality, it is your desire for God and your capacity to reach for more of God than you have right now that is the deepest essence of who you are.... Here God's Spirit dwells with our spirit, and here our truest desires make themselves known.[16]

If not desire for God, what is it you have tended to think of as the truest thing about you, the thing that defines who you are?

How does it shift your self-understanding to think of your desire for God as the truest thing about you?

In what ways do you long to be loved by God? Transformed by God? To reach for more of God?

How do these longings for God help you to understand what is most essential and true about you and who you are in God?

> The desperate desire of my heart is to navigate through the maze of this messy world to find the One who loves me as I long to be loved.
>
> *The Longing in Me*, page 161

3. Read Psalm 23, perhaps the best-known and most beloved of David's psalms. The psalm provides a beautiful picture of a soul securely at rest in the God who satisfies all longings. "The LORD is my shepherd," David writes, "I have all that I need" (Psalm 23:1). As you read the psalm, allow yourself to rest in the truth of it—the truth that God is with you in every circumstance, whether green pastures or dark valleys, and that His goodness and love follow you—now and all the days of your life. Then write your own prayer, expressing your love for God and your longing to know Him more.

_____

_____

_____

_____

_____

_____

_____

_____

_____

_____

_____

_____

_____

_____

_____

_____

_____

_____

_____

_____

About the Author

Sheila Walsh is a powerful communicator, Bible teacher, and bestselling author with more than five million books sold. A keynote speaker with Women of Faith for twenty years, Sheila has reached more than five million women by combining honesty, vulnerability, and humor with God's Word.

She is the author of *Five Minutes with Jesus*, *The Storm Inside*, and *Loved Back to Life*, and the Gold Medallion nominee for *The Heartache No One Sees*. The *Gigi, God's Little Princess* book and video series has won the National Retailer's Choice Award twice and is the most popular Christian brand for young girls in the United States. Sheila cohosted *The 700 Club* and her own show *Heart to Heart with Sheila Walsh*.

@SheilaWalsh

facebook.com/sheilawalshconnects

Sheilawalsh1

Notes

1. Alex Luc, "(*lēb, lēbāb*) heart," *New International Dictionary of Old Testament Theology and Exegesis*, vol. 2, Willem A. VanGemeren, gen. ed. (Grand Rapids: Zondervan, 1997), 749.

2. Brennan Manning, *The Furious Longing of God* (Colorado Springs: David C. Cook, 2009), 76.

3. C. S. Lewis, *The Problem of Pain* (San Francisco: HarperOne, 1940, 1996), 151, 154, 155.

4. Dallas Willard, *Knowing Christ Today: Why We Can Trust Spiritual Knowledge* (San Francisco: HarperOne 2009), 20.

5. Eugene H. Peterson, *Leap Over a Wall: Earthy Spirituality for Everyday Christians* (San Francisco: Harper-SanFrancisco, 1997), 40.

6. Dallas Willard, "Death to Self," www.dwillard.org/resources/willardwords/asp. Accessed December 6, 2015.

7. Dallas Willard, quoted in Gary W. Moon, *Eternal Living* (Downers Grove, Ill.: InterVarsity Press, 2015), 237.

8. John Piper, *Desiring God: Meditations of a Christian Hedonist*, rev. ed. (Colorado Springs: Multnomah, 2011), 4, 170.

9. Eugene H. Peterson, *The Contemplative Pastor: Returning to the Art of Spiritual Direction* (Grand Rapids: William B. Eerdmans, 1989), 31–32.

10. Walther Günther, "Grow," *New International Dictionary of New Testament Theology*, vol. 2, Colin Brown, gen. ed. (Grand Rapids: Zondervan, 1976, 1986), 128.

11. Dallas Willard, "Grace," www.dwillard.org/resources/willardwords/asp. Accessed December 18, 2015.

12. Dallas Willard, *Renovation of the Heart: Putting on the Character of Christ* (Colorado Springs: NavPress, 2002), 94.

13. Leslie C. Allen, *Psalms 101–150*, Word Biblical Commentary, vol. 21, David A. Hubbard and Glenn W. Barker, gen. eds. (Nashville: Thomas Nelson, 2002), 365.

14. Christopher A. Thurber, PhD, quoted in Derrick Ho, "Homesickness Isn't Really about Home," August 16, 2010, cnn.com. Accessed December 19, 2015.

15. Henri J.M. Nouwen, *The Return of the Prodigal Son: A Story of Homecoming* (New York: Doubleday, 1992, 1994), 106–107.

16. Ruth Haley Barton, *Sacred Rhythms: Arranging Our Lives for Spiritual Transformation* (Downers Grove, Ill.: InterVarsity Press, 2006), 24.

We long to be chosen.

We long to have control.

We long for happiness.

We long to be loved.

We long to know God cares for us.

We long to know that we matter.

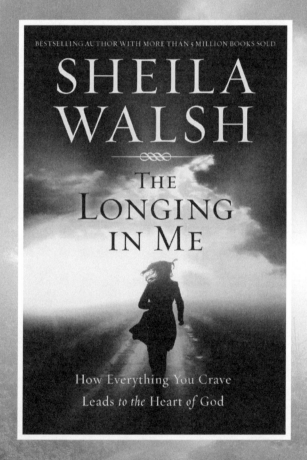